WELCOME

'The past is a foreign country: they do things differently there.' So runs the opening line of LP Hartley's 1953 novel, *The Go-Between*, a reminder, it transpires, that childhood is not without embarrassment, love is rarely straightforward and society's mores are forever changing.

The past, many would accept, is also an imperfect country, one where mistakes are inevitable, wires get entangled and opportunities – for both good and ill – go begging. So, why do so many, when looking back, send up howls of 'I should have known better' or 'I should have done better'?

It isn't the case for everyone, of course. Some will gloss over difficulties, seeing the past through rose-coloured spectacles, while others will view it more objectively. But for those with a tendency to focus on the negative, the self-reproach and lack of self-forgiveness is sometimes startling. No matter the complexity of a situation, the knowledge to hand or the sincerity of intention, they won't cut themselves any slack.

Yet to forgive, both oneself and others, is human. And it can offer hope, even during the darkest of times, making the dawn of another day seem bearable if not yet manageable. It doesn't mean forgetting and it isn't an offer of absolution (if, indeed, one is required), but it might, in time, provide a way to move on. The past, after all, is a reflection in the rear-view mirror of an ever-changing and imperfect present that whizzes by relentlessly. On occasions when it hoves into view, try to see the whole picture – and remember everyone, including you, deserves kindness.

COVER ARTIST

Scarlet Spring by Katherine of Space Frog Designs. Her passion for nature is the core influence of her work. She is fascinated by complex and simple relationships between colours, shapes and textures, often adding a touch of metallic. Find out more at spacefrogdesigns.com.

CONTENTS

BREATHE ISSUE 41

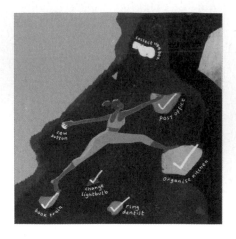

Breathe (ISSN 2397-9747) is published by
GMC Publications Ltd, 86 High Street,
Lewes, East Sussex BN7 1XN

Tel: +44 (0) 1273 477374

For editorial enquiries, email:
hello@breathemagazine.com

**For article and illustration
submissions, go to**:
breathemagazine.com/submissions

Editorial: Catherine Kielthy,
Samhita Foria, Jane Roe
Design: Jo Chapman
Marketing: Anne Guillot, Mario Perez
Production: Jim Bulley, Scott Teagle
Publisher: Jonathan Grogan
Distribution: Seymour Distribution Ltd
Printer: Precision Colour Printers

Subscription enquiries:
T: +44 (0) 1273 488005 or
pubs@thegmcgroup.com

To subscribe online, go to:
breathemagazine.com/subscribe

DON'T MISS YOUR NEXT ISSUE, ON SALE FROM 14 OCTOBER

MINDFULNESS

CREATIVITY

ESCAPE

'To free us from the expectations of others, to give us back to ourselves
– there lies the great, singular power of self-respect'

Joan Didion

The joy of inconvenience

For all the benefits gained by time-saving inventions, there's much to be said for going back to basics

I crumbled the cube into the ceramic bowl, added a few drops of water and mixed it up, creating a thick paste the colour of sunsets. As I tried to tickle out the lumps, it struck me this was way more inconvenient than squeezing a tube and slathering it on my face. I was making a face mask, not painting a masterpiece. But I also noticed how absorbed I was – watching the colour and texture change. There was something joyful in doing something so inefficient.

You've probably read ad nauseam that you should be more mindful. It makes sense. 'Mindfulness is active engagement in the moment. It puts you in the present, which makes what you're doing more pleasurable. And research shows mindfulness can reduce stress, improve memory, reduce accidents, improve relationships, and make the things you create better,' says Ellen Langer, mindfulness expert and professor in the psychology department at Harvard University.

But it can be tricky to be mindful when everyday tasks (for those with relatively affluent lifestyles) are so fast, so simple, so... convenient. Take making a cuppa. There's actually a lot to marvel over in it (this grew in Darjeeling? Where exactly is that?) – but it's probably brewed before there's a chance to do so. 'The basic tasks of our daily lives are perhaps richer and more complex than they seem because of the ways we – "we" being those in relatively wealthy western nations – have made them more convenient,' suggests Michelle Boulous Walker, associate professor in philosophy at the University of Queensland, Australia, who explores the idea of slowness through her work.

Being able to do tasks on autopilot is useful, but you also stand to lose something suggests Willem Kuyken, professor of mindfulness and psychological science at University of Oxford in the UK. 'The philosopher [Ludwig] Wittgenstein talks about this in relation to language. He says the minute we give language to something we change it and lose some of its essence. For example, when you tell a child "that's a spider's web" they never see that object again because they just assume they all look the same. And that applies to activities in our everyday lives. If you regularly buy a takeaway coffee from the same place you tend to experience it as "a cup of coffee from a certain chain", as opposed to engaging with the detail – the smell, the taste, the effect it has on your body.'

Back to basics

Perhaps this threat to mindful engagement is one of the reasons why there are pockets of resistance to hyper-convenience springing up. Film photography, with its seemingly less practical way of taking snaps and built-in element of anticipation, has been reported to be making a comeback. Interestingly, digital natives are among those reported to be taking it up as a hobby. Similarly, some travel companies are beginning to eschew flying in favour of trips by train, boat and bike and build in detours recommended by locals. And the recent trend for DIY sourdough bread, which shows no sign of waning, turns having a piece of toast into a three-day affair.

So, could there be benefits to leading a life less convenient? Of course, not everyone has that luxury. 'It used to be a sign of prosperity to have convenience foods, for example, now it's quite the opposite,' says Michelle. 'Now, in western society, it's a question of who has the time and resources not to always rely on convenience products.' Even so, no one is advocating stripping away all the advances of modern living. But what

about simple changes? Switching that teabag for loose leaf, for example, and effectively complicating the task, might increase the likelihood that you'll actively engage with the process. Less convenient might even equal more fun.

Michelle adds that there are also ethical benefits to consider. 'Take making the face mask. Once you break it down to its constituent parts you start to ask questions, such as, "Where did they come from?" or "Who made them?" and "At what cost to that person?" When I look at the term convenience, my first question would be, "For who?" Think about smartphones and all the convenience they provide. What's the cost to those who have to mine the materials for making them?'

It also raises questions about the impact these products have on the environment and, arguably, our humanity. GPS, for example, stops you getting lost, but if you never get lost, do you lose something else? 'You can see that as a metaphor for life,' says Michelle. 'If we're aimed only at convenience, and immediate success, we're going to miss what it means to be human – dealing with a circuitous path through life that will, at times, feel successful and at times absolutely not.'

In a similar way, the inconvenience of delving deeper into an issue than a news headline on a smartphone, can bring increased understanding and awareness, if not always joy. Yet going beyond the superficial, says Michelle, helps to sustain the attention without which it's almost impossible to understand the world around us and to 'deal ethically with what's happening in it'. This, of course, might take time. You might have to wait for pages to load (shock horror) or for sources to be verified. 'The idea of inconvenience seems to be attached to an idea that waiting is somehow a problem,' says Michelle. 'We lose the sense there could be any possible benefits to waiting, which seems destructive.'

The ongoing pandemic has also raised questions around convenience. It has been interesting to see so many of those who have the time and resources drawn to taking more circuitous routes to tasks – whether that's been baking bread or growing fruit and vegetables. Perhaps one reason is that for some it affords more chances for connection. You can order a loaf of bread in your weekly online shop, for example, or you can opt instead to buy flour from a local baker and call your mum for her go-to recipe. These so-called inconvenient approaches to tasks also enhance the mind and body connection, as Oxford University's Willem explains: 'There's this wonderful quote in James Joyce's *Dubliners*, "Mr Duffy lived a short distance from his body" and I think we learn to live a short distance from our bodies in modern western society,' he says. 'But when you're mixing ingredients with your hands, you're feeling them, smelling them, your mind is drawing on all this information from the body and again that can help you to stay in touch with your experience.'

On a basic level, the inconvenient route could lead to more pleasurable outcomes. Home-made meals mean you get to have them exactly to suit your palate rather than the one-taste-fits-all options on the supermarket shelves. Of course, there's also the risk it might go wrong, which would be inconvenient, but they might also be way better than you ever imagined – and therein lies the joy.

Words: Jessica Powell

INJECT SOME DIFFICULTY

Read a complex novel. 'We tend to avoid complex texts, but it brings about a slower approach to reading and is an excellent way of training ourselves back into a more attentive mode,' suggests Michelle.

Blend your own tea. Study the different ingredients, measure them out and test how they affect the final brew. Your regular cup of tea could become a ritual (see issue 12). 'Taste it as you're going along to understand how each ingredient changes the flavour,' says Ellen. 'The act of noticing is the essence of mindfulness.'

Embrace the unpredictable. Turn off the GPS and try navigating with a traditional map (see issue 40). You might go awry, but that could bring its own adventure. As Michelle notes: 'There's the oft-told tale of "I got lost, but in getting lost I discovered a whole new place".'

In your own time

Boring, mundane tasks with no deadline are often the greatest obstacles to productivity and completing bigger, more important jobs. But what if there was a way to keep on top of these small nuisances without giving them too much precious brain space? Introducing, the power hour method...

When looking for new and interesting ways to encourage productivity in daily life, it can be difficult to find methods that are quick and easy to implement. Many self-help guides encourage you to spend time meticulously journalling or planning out your days, often resulting in more time spent preparing instead of actually doing. And while planning can create a sense of purpose and motivation, it often doesn't encompass those small, awkward tasks that slip through the net of productivity. From changing that lightbulb that stopped working months ago to filling out that form you've quietly ignored, there is a method of tricking yourself into completing those nuisance tasks.

The power hour method, invented by author Gretchen Rubin, sets aside 60 minutes, once a week, to steadily work through a list of small, mildly unpleasant tasks. Within this window, Gretchen encourages you to focus on jobs that have 'no deadline, no accountability, no pressure', as these are often the ones that go unaddressed. To begin, you first create a to-do list of tasks you've been putting off. Rather than sitting and directly taking time to write it out, it could be that you add to this list over the course of the week as things crop up. Either way, putting these nuisance tasks on paper is a great way to free up space in your mind.

Once this is completed, you can begin by setting aside one hour a week where you feel most productive. This will depend entirely on you, your work routine and other commitments, and whether you are an early bird or a night owl. Whatever your requirements, this method can be slotted into your current lifestyle and requires little effort in achieving positive change. Through the power hour method, there's a quiet empowerment in completing chores that solely benefit you, particularly ones that usually get left behind. In fact, it's often the energy of having it remain uncompleted that is more stressful than the actual job itself. Setting aside this small amount of time to tick off these nagging tasks allows you to conserve your energy for the things that really matter.

Success and mindset coach Victoria Watson is an advocate for this method of productivity. She says: 'We all suffer [from] procrastination on some level and it's often the smaller, perhaps more mundane, tasks without a specific deadline that we then "add to the pile" or to the bottom of the to-do list. The problem with this is that without the deadline there isn't the motivation to get them done and we focus on the more pressing things, but then the pile of "little things" just gets bigger.' Victoria suggests that getting into the habit of setting aside 60 minutes each week can have a positive impact on emotional and mental wellbeing. She explains: 'Creating sustainable habits helps us to feel like we are in control of our lives and therefore we develop more trust in ourselves. As humans we thrive best with order and regularity. If we're putting off tasks continually, our procrastination habit becomes like a safety blanket that we don't want to shed. We get comfortable with our behaviour and it becomes harder to change it.'

Within Gretchen's work is the suggestion that paying specific attention to small problems like this can pave the way in empowering individuals to deal with bigger, life-changing decisions. Victoria has seen this in her own coaching practice, discussing how the power hour allows individuals to take on new challenges: 'By dealing with small problems in this way, we are setting the tone and creating the success foundations for our future experiences. It goes back to developing our sense of self and a big part of this is being able to rely on and trust ourselves. The more we deal with things head on, the more we develop this and our ability to deal with bigger life-changing issues which might crop up.'

Someone who has experienced the life-changing impact of the power hour is *Breathe* reader, Liam*, for whom the method helped in tackling larger obstacles: 'In dealing with the smaller,

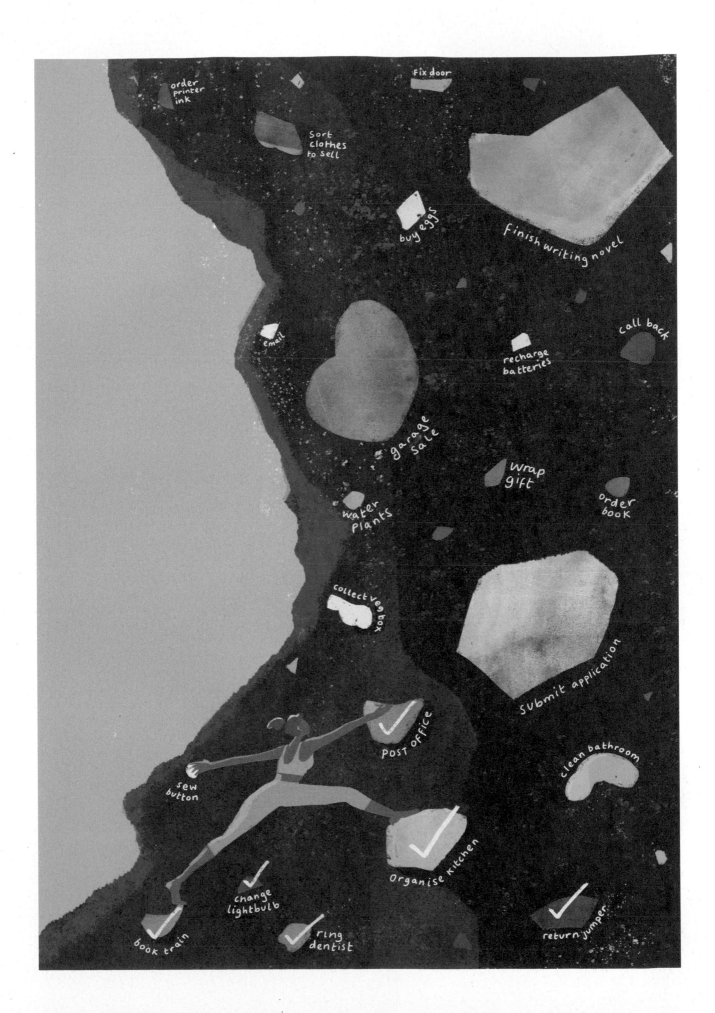

nagging issues in my day to day, it gave my mind the free space to consider other things, and think about the parts of my life I had come to neglect. As I began the weekly process, I found myself more motivated and more open to challenging the other aspects that needed more attention, such as my physical fitness.

While the method has great benefits in overcoming day-to-day obstacles to productivity, it also has potential to break negative emotional cycles. As explained by Vicki Uwannah, a chartered counselling psychologist and co-founder of the Untamed Collective, the method can be used to lift low mood: 'When depressed, individuals no longer find pleasure in previously enjoyed activities, and also stop engaging in tasks that feel difficult or challenging. To interrupt that cycle, therapists encourage clients to proactively complete activities that make them feel good about themselves.'

In aiming to be productive, while not giving into the pressure to do it all, many of us are faced with the risk of burnout. However, Vicki explores how the power hour has the potential to prevent burnout, as it forces us to consider productivity in a more nuanced way: 'Tasks that gradually mount up can be instrumental in us feeling an increased loss of control over our surroundings, our schedules and ultimately our lives. When we feel continuously burned out we are at greater risk of becoming anxious or depressed, and losing connection with things or people that usually make us feel grounded.

'So, by tricking our brains to think that we have only to put in a small amount of effort or time (for example, 60 minutes), in order to achieve difficult tasks (an ever-growing

to-do list), we're convincing ourselves that this is a manageable feat, and thus avoiding burnout.' In this way, the power hour allows us to gain back a sense of pleasure and achievement, even when we are at our lowest.

For Sara*, who has anxiety and depression, the method has allowed her to regain a sense of productivity even when she's facing challenging days: 'When I'm struggling with my mental health, I get into negative cycles of neglecting self-care and often fail to motivate myself for long stretches of time. With the power hour, I can allot time on days I feel better and more motivated, so that I can have the mental space to rest and care for myself on more difficult days. Even completing a few short tasks over the course of an hour can feel really rewarding.'

Overall, the method seems to be an effective, and empowering tool, encompassing all aspects of productivity. At times of high productivity, the 60 minutes can be used to face small, nagging tasks that take up unnecessary brain space. At times of low motivation, when there's a struggle to feel a sense of accomplishment, it has the potential to inject some much-needed productivity, even when it feels most challenging.

Words: **Hope Talbot**

To find out more about Vicki and The Untamed Collective, visit theuntamedcollective.com and @itsdrvicki on Instagram. To learn more about Victoria's work, go to victoriajanewatson.com.

ILLUSTRATIONS: AMY KATE WOLFE. * NAMES CHANGED

WHAT CAN YOU DO IN 60 MINUTES?

Clear out old clothes and upcycle jaded items. This can often be a tricky one, and occasionally requires ruthlessness when choosing what needs to be thrown away. A power hour could be used to target specific rooms or items that you need to sort through, rather than having to dedicate a whole afternoon to clearing out everything in one go.

Organise a food cupboard. Food waste and planning can be an awkward issue to face, particularly if you dread the trip to the supermarket. A quick attempt at organising and cleaning even just one food-storage space can help you think more clearly about what you're wasting, and help save you money in the long run.

Update work records. For freelancers and small businesses especially, updating financial records is essential, but it can be something that's easily ignored for months on end. By setting aside time as part of your weekly power hour, it can help make the process less daunting.

Book appointments. Whether it's for health, a haircut or a beauty treatment, booking appointments is something which can be constantly put off for another day. But this short, nagging task can be transformed into a moment to prioritise your self-care, all in the space of 60 minutes.

Fix and replace household items. In every home, it feels like there is always something that is just about getting by. Whether it's the wobbly chair, or the broken appliance or the unloved item that has been gathering dust in a corner, these things all need replacing and repairing at some point. By allocating them a space in your power hour, you can make your everyday environment a much more efficient place to be.

Get into the groove

Exploring the ancient Vedic philosophy of samskaras and how its power can be harnessed for growth in the modern day

Samskaras is a concept from ancient Indian philosophy and is significant within religions such as Jainism, Buddhism and Hinduism. While the exact mechanism of how our samskaras affect us on a subconscious level varies between different schools of thought, it's acknowledged to be closely related to karmic theory, which is that every action, intent and attitude of an individual has a direct effect on them. The word itself comes from the Sanskrit sam, 'complete or joined together' and kara, 'action, cause or doing'.

Southampton-based yoga teacher Meeta Raichura explains that 'samskaras are individual impressions created in our mind and thoughts by our own actions'. They come about as a result of habits, ideas or actions, and can be positive or negative. Together, they make up our conditioning. If thoughts and actions make up rivers rushing along the brain's landscape, our samskaras are the depressions or valleys formed. Deeper grooves are created by repetition of certain thoughts or actions, making them easier to do, just as it becomes easier for water to flow over time through a well-worn river pathway, as it's the path of least resistance.

Meeta says: 'It's similar to when you're doing yoga. When transitioning into a new pose, if you go into it really quickly, without bringing awareness and intention to it, and don't do it correctly, this creates a bad posture which could be harmful to your body. Conversely, if you slow down and go into the posture with full awareness, then you'll be getting the positive aspects of it.' In this way, if you keep repeating the bad posture, you're more likely to keep doing so in the future, whereas the more you practise the correct positioning, the more likely you will continue with proper form.

So, are we in control of our samskaras or are they in control of us? Well, it's a little like a feedback loop that begins at our spiritual birth. The belief goes that we carry our samskaras into each new birth unless we find a way to shed ones we no longer want or need. It's a philosophy that can be useful whether a person believes in reincarnation or not, too, as it suggests they can exert control over their destiny. It's also a reminder to think closely before behaving in ways that might not best serve your interests, assuming, that is, that you're aware of them.

Science of the spiritual

If this all sounds a bit abstract, fear not, because neuroscience itself has widely accepted this philosophy, just under a different, more technical name: neuroplasticity. This is the understanding that our brains are plastic. This means they're malleable and changeable according to our experiences, thoughts and beliefs – sound familiar? The influential Canadian psychologist Donald Hebb's groundbreaking 1949 theory of 'neurons that fire together, wire together' underpins this idea. Simply put, this means the brain cells that communicate together the most often, through repetition or habits, have the strongest connections between them. Hebbian theory, as it's called, connected the dots between psychology and biology, overhauling understanding of how habits and their related behaviours are produced. This is also what's behind automatic behaviours, which can be useful – reading, driving and riding a bike – and sometimes not so much – anxiety pathways, unhelpful emotional responses or unwanted habits.

And that's not the only catchy phrase associated with this idea. Another, perhaps more familiar, saying is 'practice make

perfect'. According to a study authored by Swedish psychologist and researcher Anders Ericsson, it takes on average 10,000 hours of deliberate practice to master a skill. This idea was popularised by US journalist Malcolm Gladwell, who writes in his book *Outliers – The Story of Success* that 'ten thousand hours is the magic number of greatness'. While there's much debate over the accuracy of the number itself and limitations to the study's findings, there's no doubt that lots of practice will make doing something feel more natural, compared to none at all. And this is just one of the ways you can strengthen your positive samskaras.

Force of habit

New habits and thought patterns can be hard and take time to create, as a study, headed by health psychology researcher Phillippa Lally at University College London, showed all too clearly. It described how, on average, it takes more than two months before a new behaviour becomes automatic, or 66 days to be exact (though this varies depending on the behaviour, the person and the circumstances). That might be all well and good, but it's too simplistic to say you can change your samkaras through the power of practice alone. Most patterns and behaviours are intangible and happen unconsciously, but there are other ways to cultivate more self-awareness (see right),

which can be helpful when deciding the impressions you'd like to keep and the ones you'd rather lose.

In fact, breaking or dropping habits that no longer serve you can be just as difficult as building new ones, and it becomes harder with time. The phrase 'you can't teach an old dog new tricks' might be a well-worn metaphor and generalisation, but there's some truth in the belief that long-held habits or mindsets are the most challenging to change. This is because their very repetition results in deeper, more well-travelled associated grooves in the brain. Going back to the river example and how the water goes down the path of least resistance (the well-travelled route), the same thing happens with thoughts and neural connections in the brain.

It can be difficult to change your samskaras, but it's not impossible. There are methods to open up your mind and bring awareness to your actions (see right), which become easier with regular practice. In this way, you can form fresh samskaras while shedding those that no longer serve you, and exert control over what you take into your future.

Words: **Samhita Foria**

For more on Meeta and her classes, visit meetayoga.com.

TIME FOR NEW IMPRESSIONS?

Try some or all of the following for the greatest chance of success

Yoga
The slowing down and reflection brought on by the practice allows greater awareness of the body and the mind's thoughts. The acts of letting go and using intention are both important skills that, with practice, transfer to the context of samskaras.

Meditation
Studies have shown it can increase grey matter in the brain's prefrontal cortex – this region is larger in meditators compared to in non-practitioners. This part of the brain is responsible for executive functions, such as logic, reason, willpower, creativity, decision-making, problem solving and goal setting. It also plays a role in self-awareness.

Tapping into the senses
Connecting a new habit or thought to as many areas of the brain as possible helps to develop new neural pathways. By engaging all the senses as best you can, the new behaviour gets a stickiness that helps boost its staying power.

Visualisation
Studies have shown that visualising tasks activates the same parts of the brain as does physically carrying them out. In this way, imagining yourself participating in a behaviour or habit you'd like to do more of will help to form new pathways and deepen existing ones, which all goes towards changing behaviour.

Gratitude
It's widely accepted in psychology that positive reinforcement is an effective tool for behaviour change, so harnessing the power of positivity through practising gratitude alongside your habit or thought change can be an effective tool for it to stick.

'Between stimulus and response there is a space. In that space is our power to choose our response. In our response lies our growth and our freedom'

VIKTOR FRANKL

ILLUSTRATIONS: IRINA PERJU

Start slow

Go hard or go home. No pain, no gain. Just do it. The all-or-nothing approach to success is so dominant that it's easy to forget there are other ways to prosper

I never liked running. So, when my physiotherapist suggested taking it up to reduce back pain from a previous career in figure skating, I wasn't overjoyed. Undeterred, however, he said to start slowly, to run between two markers, and build from that point. With this quiet encouragement, I decided to try again. And I did start slowly. Some would say it was walking pace. I refused the inner urge to go faster. I would stop if I felt an unusual twinge. No pain, no gain? More like no pain, no pain.

But beginning gently and building up almost imperceptibly proved effective. The physical benefits soon became apparent. As Buckinghamshire-based sports and rehabilitation therapist Jav Asaro, who is also my physio, says: 'Where appropriate, running can be a great exercise for strengthening and providing positive effects on intervertebral discs, core, diaphragm, pelvic floor and postural muscle.' But there was an unexpected outcome, too. Maintaining fitness became more manageable and enjoyable. It seemed as though the method had needed changing rather than the sport. The running was fine and keeping going created a sense of relief. The process wasn't stressful or demoralising but fun and exciting.

For some, it could be that a gentler introduction or reintroduction into physical activity can be as beneficial, if not more so, than an intense approach. 'Properly timed progressions are the quickest and most effective way to make physical gains for anyone starting or transitioning back into physical activity,' says former Rugby League player and Bradford City FC commercial director Davide Longo. A suitable programme will take into account various factors, such as skill level, previous injury and personal goals. Arguably, a lighter introduction and run-in aren't always given equal consideration. Yet if this helps to lead to a sustained exercise routine, it can also bring psychological benefits such as reduced anxiety, better sleep and a general boost in mood.

With a more relaxed attitude, stress and fatigue from overdoing an activity might also be minimised, which could make it easier to stick with a routine and increase motivation and staying power. Kala Flynn, a life coach, consultant and author from Milton Keynes, explains: 'Avoid limiting yourself to [bigger goals such as] "I'll be happy once I've run a marathon." You can get just as much fulfilment from an extended walk and taking in nature's surroundings, birds and trees. In those moments, enhancing your awareness of what you're seeing, hearing and feeling, is enough to stimulate your senses and

wake up the cells in your body.' It's an approach that aligns more closely with a broader view of success, 'the accomplishment of an aim or purpose'. Considered within this dictionary definition, success can be measured as a daily stroll to the local store as much as the winning of an Olympic gold medal.

Trying a new sport, or returning to one, can be daunting, especially if there's pressure to go all-in and give it everything you've got. The exhortation to go hard or go home will undoubtedly work for some, but it's not a universal solution. 'If you go from one extreme to the other, you can end up burning out without even realising it,' says Kala. 'It's good just to keep moving rather than not doing anything at all. You don't have to see the whole staircase to take the first step.' Put like this, it's also possible to see how the start-slowly approach can apply as equally to writing a novel or pursuing a new career path, as it might to improved fitness. You just need to break it down and consider that every aspect of the task, no matter how imperceptible, will take you a fraction further. Here are a few things you might try:

- *Want to be a bit healthier? Just do five star jumps or press-ups a day for a week and then try it for a month or two.*
- *Want to draw more cartoons? Sketch one every Tuesday when you have a spare minute.*
- *Struggling to write an article? Compose a couple of sentences or one paragraph twice a week and see where it goes.*
- *Want to progress in your career? Email one contact this week.*

It seems contradictory to think doing less can become more. But breaking down tasks into bite-sized pieces might be the key to sustaining progress and getting further. Of course, there's no one-size-fits-all approach and to perform or create anything at a high level requires work, but there's no shame in starting slowly.

I thought I could never run. I was about to give up on it entirely. But now I've realised I can do it, my way. I can run for 18 minutes now, three times a week, consistently, with no thoughts of giving up. And I've kept that up for three months, smashing my past record, which was, sadly, somewhere around the two-week mark. I know 18 minutes isn't a marathon, but it's something, and it counts. So, next time there's a task to tackle, try focusing on that first small step.

Words: Lizzie Matcham

Digital chat

Email can be fun, useful or annoying in equal parts, so it's wise to stop and think before clicking send on messages – including the well-intentioned ones

Email is such an integral part of daily life it's hard to imagine how people managed without it. It's been growing ever since the late-1990s and, despite rumours of its demise, email for business and personal use is not going away any time soon. As useful as it is, however, there are drawbacks. Have you ever considered how much of your time is spent replying to emails from friends and colleagues? And have you noticed how some people seem to be replacing one-on-one work banter with chatty correspondence instead? Some even choose to send emails to colleagues across the room rather than walking over to speak to them.

It can also drain personal reserves. Does your heart sink when you're trying to concentrate on a project and yet another message from a well-meaning contact flashes up, asking about your day or your plans for the weekend? Conversations that could take minutes face to face can end up being stretched out over a dozen emails in an exchange that punctuates your whole day. Of course, there'll always be a place for warm, friendly and interesting emails in building and strengthening professional and personal relationships. But with the average worker spending almost a third of their day checking and answering messages in their inbox, according to a study by McKinsey Global Institute, how do you know when to pause a digital conversation or let the thread drop?

Making small talk via email can be a useful way of staying up to date with friends and colleagues when you aren't able to see them in person. It has more value than bland, impersonal communications and contacts will likely respond well to the person who remembers to ask on a Monday morning how their daughter's birthday weekend went or how the house sale is going. But it's important to know where to draw the line. Often emails can bounce back and forth with short sentences, emojis or 'lols', just because people feel under pressure to reply.

Trine Syvertsen, professor of media studies at the University of Oslo, has written a book called *Digital Detox: The Politics of Disconnecting*. She says that when email was initially introduced, it was welcomed as something that would save time and reduce the need for too many meetings. Now the tables have turned and, based on her research and interviews with digital-media users, she believes what people find most irritating or intrusive is email checking. 'We see it as a social obligation and feel we have to reply,' she says. 'We forget that there is someone on the other end and their time is valuable too. If you're not careful you can end up in a cycle of being interrupted, and interrupting others.' Some European countries, including France and Germany, have introduced or are looking at bringing in laws around 'the right to disconnect', giving employees freedom to close down their work email and other communications outside office hours. It's important to remember these days, with emails arriving 24/7, trying to have an empty inbox is a near-impossible, needlessly stressful task. Sometimes you just have to step back, switch off and let go.

Trine says that as well as disconnecting or trying to limit inbox-checking to certain times of day, you might also self-regulate your own email habits by thinking about what you're bringing to the conversation. 'I try to think about sending something substantial,' she says. 'It's about adding something useful to the exchange - perhaps a suggested day or time to meet, or a resolution to a problem. I think about how to move the conversation forward so it requires a shorter thread.'

When involved in a sociable email exchange, this might be as simple as including a few details about your own day, or weekend, at the same time as you ask someone else how their day is going - so they don't feel as though they have to reciprocate by asking you the same question. And an easy way of drawing a conversation to a close is to simply stop asking questions. It's also worth considering that few people expect you to reply straight away. If you are involved in an email conversation you might feel under pressure to keep the momentum flowing, not letting that cyber tennis ball drop. But the person on the other end might not be expecting a quick response, especially if you're only exchanging pleasantries. They might even be secretly hoping you don't reply for a few hours to allow them the thinking space to focus on another task.

Author Michael Harris, from Vancouver, Canada, has written several books chronicling his own journey to a better relationship with technology. In his latest, *All We Want*, scheduled for publication in December, he suggests the problem many face is an expectation to maintain 'constant ambient connectivity', which is not necessarily focused or useful, but means they're always reachable. Email and messaging tools have effectively replaced the workplace coffee room. 'It's a

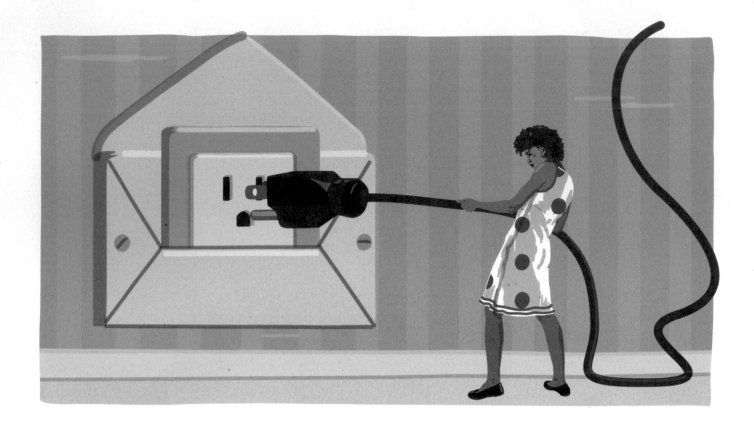

constant tide of communication but the problem is you can't see the person at the other end,' he says. 'In a physical setting, it's immediately obvious if a person is busy or concentrating and doesn't want to be disturbed. But when people are all behind screens, you have no idea what you're interrupting.'

Often you might find yourself compelled to keep an email chain going or continue replying, out of guilt or social pressure. You don't want the person on the other end to think you're ignoring them or you got bored with the conversation. But perhaps the most considerate thing to do would be to give them the mental space and time to think about something else. Michael explains: 'Every interruption destroys your ability to focus on what you're actually trying to do with your time. It takes around 15 minutes after an interruption to get back into a state of flow, so if you're checking your emails every 10 minutes you're never going to get into a flow.'

Michael suggests setting boundaries, such as removing email or work-related message apps from your phone, or stopping notifications from flashing up on your desktop, and then 'batch-processing' your emails in time blocks. He also suggests using your out-of-office message to manage other people's expectations – although take care not to set the same message all the time as there's a good chance it will lose its impact. 'You could try setting your status to advise people you're going into a period of solo working for a few hours, or a meeting, or that you won't be email checking until later in the day,' he says. 'It's like [creating] a moat around yourself to give yourself space to think.' When it comes to managing your inboxes, never lose sight of the fact that these technologies were created to make life easier – not harder. It's how you use them that counts.

Words: **Jade Beecroft**

HOW TO AVOID BECOMING AN EMAIL HOGGER

Don't always reply straight away. If the message is non-urgent, set aside time when it's convenient to respond later in the day.

Think of the other person. Keep in mind that people have many demands on their time.

Make it count. Include plenty of information in your email and try to move the conversation forward so it requires fewer responses.

Don't send 'lazy' responses. One-line emails that don't answer people's questions just mean more follow-ups are needed.

Use the out-of-office function. It's not just for holidays – you can switch it on whenever you want to manage others' expectations of how fast you'll respond.

Forget FOMO. Is the fear of missing out causing you to send replies? Try just letting things drop from time to time.

Manage your time. Try not to respond to work emails in personal time and vice versa. Set boundaries, and also have time out from being connected.

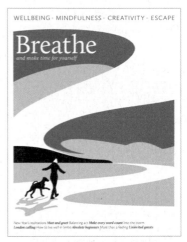

Subscribe or order back issues

VISIT BREATHEMAGAZINE.COM

CALL +44 (0)1273 488005

Past forward

Looking back, it's easy to imagine that at times you should, in the sentiment of that well-worn phrase, 'have known better'. But life is imperfect and, despite what your inner-critic might suggest, no one at any time has access to a crystal ball

Hindsight is a funny thing. Looking back, whether to 10 minutes or 10 years ago, and thinking twice about something said or done... Such a stream of consciousness can get caught up in the proverbial dam that is made up of five frustrating words: 'I should have known better.' But on retreading your footsteps, is it always the case that the first outcome must be beating yourself up? The answer is no, it isn't, and seldom is, necessary.

Let's start with what experts call creeping determinism and what I call crystal-ball syndrome: the belief that, somehow, in some way, you did in fact know back then what you know now but you were unable to put that knowledge into action. Often people are fooled into thinking in this manner, which can be the product of guilt, frustration or a lack of self-esteem. It's the point where your metaphorical foot begins to metaphorically kick your backside over something no longer within your control in the present. The moment has passed, in other words, but you're certain it could and should have gone differently had you used your head. Of course, instances arise where the correct tools to remedy a situation were to hand but slipped down a drain grate. If this happens, be kind to yourself, as hindsight can distort memories, convincing you that you knew everything (when you didn't), that you were best-placed (when you weren't) or that you understood every nuance of a situation (who's ever in that position?). The bottom line is that unless you have a time machine like Doc Brown in *Back to the Future*, or decided that day to slip up on purpose, there's an element of implausibility to this crystal-ball notion, despite the tendency to gravitate towards it. Hindsight can't always be trusted.

Important life lessons

Arguably it's more likely you were or are being naive. This has become a dirty word and, perhaps, a dirty way of being in some circles. Yet such negative connotations need to be challenged because everyone from Isaac Newton (who'd think it was a good idea to sit under an apple tree so near to harvest season, anyway?) to Leonardo da Vinci (terrific effort on designing a flying machine, don't get me wrong, but here are a few notes...) has experienced momentary lapses of reason. What's helpful to remember is that the innocence of your former self is the wisdom of your present one. This is because with experience comes better understanding, so while it might not feel nice in

real time, it provides a forward trajectory, a push in the right direction. And a nudge towards learning.

Think, for example, of the phrase 'You learn something new every day'. It's an oft-heard refrain and it's true. But it doesn't begin to scratch the surface as in reality, you learn something new every second. From one moment to the next, you're taking in information, some of which you'll be aware of and more that will exist only in the deep recesses of your mind. In each fragment of waking existence – and even when you're asleep – you're absorbing things. It's brilliant, practical and, most importantly, an ongoing and never-ending process.

Because life isn't a video game – you can't keep 'levelling up' until you max out and have nowhere else to go. When that does happen during a game, boredom quickly sets in and, inevitably, the console, computer or tablet gets turned off. Indeed, once the challenge has disappeared, every area of the map has been explored and all the bad guys have been defeated, there is little left to maintain attention. Reality is different. Humanity's gift is a capacity to develop constantly and consistently, to keep learning, not every day, but every second, to recognise mistakes, yes, but not to let them define you. It's all about allowing them to rest in the past while striving for a better future.

Even if those mistakes do for whatever reason resurface, that's okay. There's little use in repeatedly kicking yourself. If you did so, in the literal sense, your backside would become unnecessarily sore, and the same is true when speaking figuratively. Firstly, accept that similar obstacles might crop up many times on your personal track. It might take a few attempts to overcome them, but have faith that you'll do it eventually. It might be in your own style, but that's fine. After all, who decides the best way to grasp what's best for an individual's personal growth? Neither is there a three-strikes-and-you're-out limit. No matter how many times it takes, no matter how bumpy or uncomfortable those obstacles turn out to be, there's an opportunity nestled in every temporary shortcoming. For temporary is the magic word, even if it doesn't feel like it today or yesterday or every day since whatever happened took place. Your capacity to overcome is becoming stronger behind the scenes – and it'll show itself when it's ready.

Words: **Alex Bowers**

ILLUSTRATION: OLIVIA WALLER

LIVING

'Without memory, there is no culture. Without memory,
there would be no civilisation, no society, no future'

Elie Wiesel

My Family and other narratives

They're as complex as the individuals that make them up, yet the view of these inherited groups is often singular, that they're identikit units and the be-all and end-all of everything. Is there room for a more nuanced story?

Family is important. It's the first social group we belong to. Much is learned from this early unit – irrespective of its composition or boundaries – including role responsibilities, boundaries and how to negotiate with others. However, with age comes the freedom to create our own milieu.

I don't have a problem with family, many of my best times have been spent with my parents and cousins. In fact, as I sit and write these words, the days that I hanker for most are the simplest ones that involve drinking tea and eating cake with my mother and gran. But since they both passed, my family has somewhat dispersed. What once was is no more. I have found myself in an amorphous group connected by blood. And this group, comprising aunts, uncles and cousins, often does not represent me. Some of them do, as individuals, but not as the collective known as the Family.

Since some key members passed away, I've grappled with the idea of belonging. Family isn't fixed, of course, members will die and new ones will be born. It's the natural pruning of the family tree, not unlike the deadheading of a rose bush. So it stands to reason that a unit that once provided a sense of belonging or was comfortable might no longer feel like home. This all sounds rather logical and obvious, but it's a sentiment that's often followed by a societal pearl-clutching.

Spectrum of experiences

The emphatic statement that 'family is all that matters' expresses nothing more than an ideal. And while it's often true, like everything in life, it's mutable. For those who find they're more suitably fitted in other groups, with friends for example, the statement might suggest they've failed or that their feeling of misplacement among the people with whom they grew up or those who raised them is down to their inadequacy.

But families are as individual as the people who make them up. An article I read about the importance of this unit stated that family never fails you. But that's only one version, and my experience is to the contrary. The concern, however, is that sticking to this one mantra risks telling half-truths.

Arguably, if society was more honest about the spectrum of experiences individuals face with their own, people whose families don't fit them would feel less like failures. Yet there seems to be only one narrative. There's much written and said on the merits of keeping close those who are related to us,

ILLUSTRATIONS: NATASCHA BAUMGARTNER

but little about how these relationships, like any other, can sour. Divorces and friendship breakdowns are frequently and publicly unpicked, but family relationships rarely come under the same microscope. And because of this, when people have asked me about mine, I've sometimes pretended it's a perfectly functioning unit.

Telling the truth, that I'm estranged from some relatives, provokes bewilderment and judgment: 'But that's your sister/brother/aunt,' comes the reply, suggesting that relations have a licence to treat us however they wish, badly or otherwise. It also implies that we're obliged to forgive pernicious treatment at the hands of family members. The response often betrays an unwillingness to accept that sometimes these close relationships can and do break down beyond repair. And this attitude silences people like me.

I've often wondered, however, if my lack of honesty helps to perpetuate the myth that families can do no wrong. So, at times, when I feel I'm in safe company, I try to tell the truth. And surprisingly, it doesn't always garner the same disbelieving response with which I'm so familiar. In fact, many people have experienced similar family strife. Perhaps, contrary to the popular belief that 'family is all that matters', it might be closer to the truth and more of a universal experience to say 'family matters, sometimes'.

Home is where the heart is

For those who wish, there's a certain freedom in acknowledging there's no real need to cling to a family group. You can create your own milieu that's authentic to you. It's an idea that's widely practised anyway, sometimes inadvertently, when you choose who to spend time with, which clubs to enrol on and which hobbies to take up. It's not so iconoclastic to admit openly that family members aren't the people you feel most at home with. And it should be okay to acknowledge this loudly and without shame. It can be an act of bravery to admit to marching to a different beat of the drum. I have found home in many places and with many people, where truths and ideas are shared. And in these other homes, I find parts of me.

Even with my earlier declaration that my most cherished memories involve family, it's not a contradiction to say that this unit matters, sometimes. All relationships are subject to change. It takes courage to walk away from something that no longer serves you well. Change is both inevitable and essential in life. It's folly to hang on to something that once was but no longer is. It takes insight and, albeit painful, acknowledgement to know the difference. It can be a freeing revelation that allows you to paint and structure your own life. I have many homes and have lived many lives from acknowledging that family is not always the one that raises you.

UNPICKING THE TIES

- Most people have family issues, so don't feel embarrassed if your unit isn't perfect.

- Not everyone needs to know your life story. If you don't feel comfortable telling someone about your situation, don't.

- Don't feel bad if you pick and choose who you want to spend your time with. Most people don't get on with everyone, and that's normal.

- You can build your own hand-picked family, made up of friends and relations that become a supportive unit that's more reflective of you.

- Stop comparing your family with others. Yes, some are great, but most people don't openly discuss the difficulties within their unit. As the saying goes: 'You don't know what happens behind closed doors.'

- Don't let anyone ever tell you friends can't be family. They can. In fact, they can be at the heart of better relationships because you've chosen them.

- Accept your situation. It takes courage to look at things with clarity. If members of your family have hurt you more than they've shown you love, then it's okay to distance yourself from them. You don't need to cut them off, just limit your time with them. A toxic relationship is just that, whether the person is related to you or not.

- If someone in your family is not good for your mental health, don't feel obliged to continue the relationship. Understandably, some ties are easier to end than others, but there are organisations that can help, including the charity Stand Alone, which helps people deal with family estrangement. See standalone.org.uk for more information.

Words: Kiran Sidhu

Fabulously fungal

There's so much more to mushrooms than simply being a delicious kitchen staple – here we explore some of their wide-ranging uses as well as their incredible potential for the future

A tasty ingredient for a risotto or an omelette, free food to be foraged from fields or woods, a supernatural structure that springs up overnight in 'fairy rings'. While mushrooms could conjure up any or none of these suggestions, it's defined as a fungus of many varieties and two distinct types: cultivated and wild. Not to be confused with inedible, often-poisonous toadstools, mushrooms refer to common edible fungus of fields and meadows. Toadstools should always be approached with caution, but not all mushrooms are as innocent and edible as you might think either – some are poisonous, such as fly amanita or green-spored lepiota. That's why it's critical to know what you're dealing with when foraging for fungi – if you're in any doubt or can't ask an expert, don't go there.

The broader world of fungi is sometimes known as the 'third kingdom' because they're neither plants nor animals, although in terms of DNA, scientists say they're more closely related to animals. Edible mushrooms found in kitchens worldwide, that grow in woods and fields, are just the visible fruiting body of much larger organisms. This 'fruit' is a seasonal production, pushed up to spread spores out into the world. Underground is where the fungi lie, in big tentacles called mycelia, that grope below the earth in search of nutrients.

Deliciously diverse

Fans of fungi will be familiar with common edible types such as white button, chestnut, oyster, shiitake, chanterelle and portobello. Less well known include enoki, shimeji, wood blewit and maitake, while the more exotic hedgehog and king trumpet are sought out by connoisseurs. Truffles are almost a category on their own. Rare and highly prized, they refer to the fruiting body of an ascomycetous fungus, found growing underground in the shadow of oak trees, as well as hazel, fir or beech trees. They can be cultivated, but it's a long, difficult process, so they're mainly found by truffle hunters, working with female pigs and trained dogs that can sniff them out from beneath the forest floor – which is why they're one of the world's most expensive foods and considered one of the finest delicacies.

Outside of the food world, fungi have important uses – notably for wellbeing. Drugs such as penicillin and statins are produced from them, and medicinal mushrooms, such as reishi, chaga and cordyceps, are being commercially used in powders, extracts, beverages, broths, chocolates, face creams and shower gels. The world market in infused products is estimated to be worth more than £4billion and rising. Mushrooms have been put to work to clean up the environment, too, and there are even plans to build homes with them using so-called mushroom bricks via bioengineering (see panel overleaf). No wonder some people believe our future is fungal.

Certainly, they have a time-honoured place in ancient history. In traditional medicine down the ages, they have been valued for their healing properties. Around 460BCE, the Greek physician Hippocrates is said to have identified the amadou mushroom as being good for reducing inflammation. Old Chinese texts dating back to 206BCE describe reishi as an anti-ageing remedy, treasured as an 'elixir of life', while the Romans considered mushrooms to be the food of the gods. And yet in medieval times, they were regarded as sinister – or 'the fruit of the devil'. In Asia, they're widely used medicinally, with more than 100 varieties deployed for the treatment of cancer.

Health food

There's a growing awareness of the use of mushrooms to boost health. According to *BBC Good Food*, as well as having immune-supporting nutrients, all edible varieties contain protein and fibre in varying quantities, as well as B vitamins and selenium, a powerful antioxidant. They are one of the few non-animal sources of vitamin D (white button ones in particular) – you can also buy enriched mushrooms that have been exposed to ultraviolet light, or you can slice up regular ones on foil paper and put them in the open air for as little as 15 minutes to enhance their vitamin D content by a quarter.

Someone whose life, and health, has been entwined with the mushroom world is Martin Powell, a biochemist and practitioner of Chinese herbalism. He's been involved in the study of fungi – or mycology – for several decades and is the author of *Medicinal Mushrooms*, a guide to their health benefits. He says: 'Mushrooms can support healthy immune function and be beneficial for conditions characterised by immune deficiency, such as chronic or recurrent viral conditions like herpes and HPV.' A study published in October 2020 in *The Journal of Nutritional Biochemistry*, found consumption of the most commonly eaten mushrooms (such as white button and portobello) could promote health benefits including lower cancer risk, and improved immune function and

gastrointestinal health. (The study had been based on eating an average portion, or handful, of mushrooms three to five times a week.) A 2019 study by Tohoku University in Japan of more than 36,000 Japanese men over several decades suggested an association between eating mushrooms and a lower risk of prostate cancer; and in a 2020 study of 354 healthy Japanese adults, they were the food group with the greatest positive impact on gut bacterial diversity.

Deeper meanings

Martin has also founded *The Mushroom*, a magazine whose profits go to help people working with fungi 'to address the multiple challenges facing the planet and all its inhabitants'. One such person is Chido Govera, 34, from Zimbabwe. She lost her parents as a young girl and managed to escape a child marriage to train in biology and mycology. She's now a farmer, campaigner and educator in her native country. 'Mushrooms came into my life when as a little girl I struggled for food,' she tells *The Mushroom*. 'In Zimbabwe, mushroom season was a time we had really good meals.' Chido learned about mushrooms from her grandmother, who at 100 had gone blind but could tell her which types were edible or poisonous

and which could be treated so they could be eaten. 'What struck me, at 11, was how in a small, controlled environment I could farm with ease, harvest mushrooms and sell them and pay for my expenses. In this way, I started my dream of helping other orphans.' Having founded The Future of Hope Foundation, to promote cultivation as a sustainable source of food and income in poor regions, Chido now works with vulnerable local communities, especially women, helping them grow mushrooms to support themselves. She's focused on oyster varieties as they're the easiest to grow. Beyond food and income, mushrooms offer a deeper meaning for her: 'You cannot teach [people] about mushrooms without showing the interconnectedness of everything. What they're able to teach is for me very intriguing: you can see the power of community and the spirit of Ubuntu.'

In the natural world, ecosystems rely on fungi. 'Some plants cannot grow without mushrooms to help them absorb nutrients from the soil substrate they're growing in,' says Martin. He notes how they've been used in New York City to clear up environmental damage. 'As they have the ability to digest hydrocarbons, they've been used on oil spills in one area.' The botanical gardens at Kew in southwest London is a global

epicentre for mycology, as it holds the largest collection of dry fungal specimens in the world, with more than 1.25 million so far. In an issue of *Kew magazine*, Richard Wright, mycology outreach officer at the gardens, pondered which fungi he would take if he was to be stranded on a desert island – and showed how just one variety could be so versatile. 'I'd probably take the tinder polypore (*Fomes fomentarius*),' he wrote, adding that this woody bracket fungus contains a dense woolly material inside 'that will easily light with a tiny spark. This would help enormously with making fires for warmth, cooking and signalling for help if I decided to leave.' It would also make a good bowl for gathering water and food, he observed, adding: 'Tinder polpore is also known to have antiviral properties, which may come in useful.'

Without fungi, he says, we'd probably not have any plants on land – so it's unlikely there would be any land-dwelling animals either. Who'd have thought life on earth owed so much to these humble organisms?

Words: **Beverley D'Silva**

Warning: Do not eat any mushroom or fungi that has not been properly identified by a qualified professional, as some are poisonous when ingested. All edible wild fungi should be cooked before eating.

Fancy including some fantastic fungi in your cooking? Turn the page for some marvellous mushroom recipes

MAGICAL MUSHROOMS

- The white truffle (*Tuber magnatum*) is worth its weight in gold. In 2007, one found in the woods in Tuscany was bought at a charity auction for £160,000, it weighed 1.5kg. One reason it's so valuable is because it can't be cultivated – it grows naturally or not at all.

- Author and creator of *Peter Rabbit* Beatrix Potter was an amateur mycologist. She made hundreds of detailed paintings and drawings of fungi, studying them under a microscope. She wrote a paper on fungi in 1897 but as a woman, was not allowed to address the all-male Linnean Society. Her artworks have been used to identify a variety of species.

- According to the *Guinness World Records*, the Earth's largest living organism is a specimen of honey fungus (*Armillaria ostoyae*) in the form of a mycelium below ground in Oregon's Blue Mountains. It's much larger than a blue whale at 3.9km wide and equivalent to 1,350 football pitches.

- Honeybees are vulnerable to virus-carrying mites, but now entomologists at Washington State University have found that feeding colonies extract of *Ganoderma resinaceum*, diluted in sugar water, produced a 45,000-fold reduction in one common infection.

- Psilocybin – the psychoactive compound in 'magic mushrooms' – is the subject of trials at King's College London, with the aim of treating intractable forms of depression. Some participants reported a 50 per cent reduction in symptoms three months after the dose. A London-based mental-health care company has raised more than £80million to develop an antidepressant derived from this compound.

- Quick-growing oyster mushrooms produce masses of mycelia that can be moulded into building materials that are, pound for pound, stronger than concrete. Researchers at the University of the West of England are using them as the basis for a project which aims to embed living mycelium networks into mushroom houses of the future.

Room for shrooms?

Delicious? Check. Naturally plant-based?
Check. Packed with essential vitamins
and minerals? Check, check

HOT AND SOUR
WAKAME SOUP

Slightly spicy, tangy and deliciously healing,
this broth-based soup is rich in iodine (from
the wakame). Wakame is a type of kelp that is
closely related to the seaweed kombu and pairs
well with the robust flavors of ginger, garlic and
tamari. The edamame packs in some healthy soy
protein and the thinly sliced mushrooms bring
a satisfying meatiness. Serve this alongside rice
crackers for an added crunch.

SERVES 3-4

- 2 tbsp avocado oil
- ⅓ yellow onion, chopped small
- 1 tbsp fresh ginger, minced
- 2 cloves garlic, minced
- 230g mini portobello or shiitake mushrooms, thinly sliced
- ½ tsp sea salt
- ½ tsp black pepper
- ¼ tsp chilli flakes (optional)
- 1 litre low-sodium vegetable broth
- 200g edamame, shelled
- 3 tbsp wakame
- 3 tbsp rice vinegar
- 2 tbsp tamari
- 2 tbsp filtered water
- 1 tsp sesame oil
- 2 tsp tapioca flour (or arrowroot flour)
- Optional toppings: spritz of fresh lime, spring onions, chilli flakes, coriander

1. Heat the avocado oil in a large pot over medium-high heat. Once hot, add the onion and sauté until it turns translucent, 3-4 minutes. Stir in the ginger and garlic and cook 2-3 more minutes, stirring occasionally until fragrant.

2. Stir in the mushrooms, sea salt, black pepper and chilli flakes, if using. Cover the pot and steam cook, stirring occasionally for 5 minutes, or until mushrooms start to brown.

3. Pour in the vegetable broth, edamame and wakame (you will notice the wakame expands in the soup!). Bring to a slow boil, then reduce heat to simmer. Meanwhile, whisk together the rice vinegar, tamari, water, sesame oil and tapioca or arrowroot flour in a small bowl. Stir the mixture into the soup and let simmer together for 10 minutes, or until the soup is slightly thickened.

4. Spoon the soup into bowls, sprinkle with the optional toppings, and serve hot. Store leftovers in an airtight container in the refrigerator for up to 3 days, or in the freezer for up to 3 months.

BLACK RICE WINTER IMMUNITY GLOW BOWL

This immunity-boosting glow bowl has lots of bright and fresh flavours – the black rice looks so cool and has a wonderful nutty, earthy flavour, plus it's packed with iron and potassium. Mini portobellos are high in B vitamins, phosphorus, selenium and copper, but you can also use shiitake mushrooms. The cayenne pepper and apple-cider vinegar in the sauce bring additional immune-boosting properties.

SERVES 2–3

Rice bowl
- 100g dry black rice
- 230ml filtered water
- 1 tbsp avocado oil
- ⅓ yellow onion, chopped
- 1 medium-sized golden beetroot, peeled, quartered and sliced
- 230g mini portobello or shiitake mushrooms
- ½ tsp sea salt
- ½ tsp black pepper
- 100g edamame, shelled

Avocado-pumpkin seed sauce
- ½ ripe avocado
- Handful fresh coriander
- 2 tbsp pumpkin seeds
- ½ clove garlic, minced
- ½ lime, juiced
- 2 tbsp apple-cider vinegar
- 1 tbsp olive oil
- 1 tsp pure maple syrup
- ½ tsp sea salt
- ½ tsp black pepper
- ⅛ tsp ground cayenne pepper

1. Combine the black rice and water in a medium saucepan over high heat. Bring to a boil, then cover and reduce the heat to simmer for 45 minutes. Turn off the heat and keep the lid on until ready to serve.
2. Meanwhile, heat the oil in a large frying pan over medium-high heat. Once hot, add the onion and sauté until it turns translucent, 3-4 minutes. Stir in the golden beetroot and cover to steam cook for 7-8 minutes.

3. Stir in the mushrooms, sea salt and black pepper and cook 3-4 minutes, until lightly browned. Stir in the edamame and cook 3-4 minutes more to warm.
4. Combine all the ingredients for the sauce in a high-speed blender. Blend until smooth and creamy.
5. To serve, divide the rice among two or three bowls. Top each portion with some of the veggie mixture, then drizzle with the sauce. Store leftovers in an airtight container in the refrigerator for up to 3 days.

TORTILLA MUSHROOM AND 'MOZZARELLA CREAM' PIZZA

This mozzarella cream is absolutely dreamy and totally fun to make. This recipe uses a gluten-free brown rice tortilla as the base, but feel free to use whatever type of tortilla you prefer – or even real pizza dough. Sprinkle some rocket on top for extra colour and greens.

SERVES 2

Pizza
- 2 gluten-free brown rice tortillas
- 225g marinara sauce
- 1 medium tomato, sliced thinly
- 100g mushrooms, any variety, sliced thinly
- Handful of fresh basil, sliced thinly
- Optional toppings: sprinkle of chilli flakes, extra basil, fresh rocket or spinach

Mozzarella cream
- 150g raw cashews, soaked in hot water for 10 minutes, then drained and rinsed
- 230ml filtered water
- 2 tsp olive oil
- 2 tsp nutritional yeast
- 1 tsp fresh lemon juice (or apple-cider vinegar)
- 1 tsp tapioca starch
- ¾ tsp sea salt
- ¼ tsp onion powder

1. Preheat the oven to 200C/400F/gas mark 6.
2. Arrange the tortillas on two baking sheets. Make sure all the veggies are sliced and ready before making the mozzarella cream.
3. Combine all the ingredients for the mozzarella cream in a high-speed blender and blitz until smooth. The mixture will seem watery. If your blender is not high speed and some small chunks of cashews remain, pour the cream through a fine-mesh strainer or nut-milk bag to remove them.
4. Pour the mozzarella cream into a medium saucepan over medium-high heat. Using a spatula, continuously stir, scraping down the sides and bottom, for 4-5 minutes, or until it begins to thicken and get stretchy. Then turn off the heat and let cool.
5. Spread a thin layer of marinara sauce over the top of each tortilla, then add dollops of mozzarella cream.
6. Layer with the tomatoes, mushrooms and fresh basil.
7. Bake for 16-20 minutes, or until the edges are golden and crispy. Let cool for 2-3 minutes and then slice into quarters.
8. Store leftover pizza in the refrigerator for up to 2 days. If you have leftover mozzarella cream, store it in the refrigerator for up to 2 days. To use, reheat it slowly in a saucepan, adding a few teaspoons of water if it seems too thick.

Edited extract from The Plant-based Cookbook for Women *by Shannon Leparski, Blue Star Press, RRP £25.99. Available online and in bookshops.*

PHOTOGRAPHS: SHANNON LEPARSKI

Special perks

Italy is synonymous with delicious coffee, from creamy cappuccinos to gorgeous granitas. But what do rituals and timing have to do with its role as a coffee-culture world leader?

Spend any length of time in Italy and you can't help but notice how different the coffee-drinking rituals can be there. This is not to say all Italians are dependent on their morning cappuccino, or that you won't see oat milk or even the occasional pumpkin-spiced latte being drunk with gusto. It's more that the joy of drinking coffee is deep-rooted in Italian culture. In cafés, homes and crumbling piazzas, these traditions are a part of daily life, from Florence to Naples, Turin to Milan.

According to Italian coffee company Illy, almost 97 per cent of Italians drink the brew in some form. 'In Italy, we are characterised by our love of espresso, but now we're open to many other ways of drinking coffee,' says Moreno Faina, the director of Illy's Università del Caffè in Trieste, set up in 1999

to promote 'the culture of high-quality coffee'. 'Drinking a coffee is a moment of relaxation and joy and happiness,' he says. 'I could talk about it for hours.'

Over the page we look at some of the country's coffee rituals and discover that when it comes to enjoying the drink, the Italians really do know a thing or two. It's worth noting, though, that drinking coffee like an Italian isn't about puritanical rules. The sheer variety is proof the preparation doesn't have to be traditional to capture the country's ethos. But however you drink yours, taking time to savour the process can add a little calm to daily life.

Turn over to explore more about Italy's unique coffee culture

The breakfast cappuccino

A cappuccino at breakfast time, often enjoyed with a cornetto (the Italian version of the croissant) or biscotti (a hard biscuit), is still popular all across Italy. The idea is that the drink's dairy- or plant-milk content will fill you up until lunchtime. However, it seems that indulging in a mid-morning pastry as well is no bad thing. According to custom, a cappuccino should only be drunk before lunch, after which time espresso takes over.

The post-lunch espresso

In Naples, espresso is often served with a small glass of water. This is not, as is commonly thought, to wash away the bitter taste of the coffee after drinking it. Quite the opposite: according to Neapolitan tradition the flavour should be savoured, and the water is meant to cleanse your palate ahead of your first sip of coffee, so you can appreciate it to the full. After lunch, espressos can be drunk quickly at the bar, or more leisurely in a piazza. Espresso macchiato topped with a little frothed milk is another favourite. Illy's Moreno, meanwhile, is partial to a capo – an espresso in a glass with a few drops of milk.

The moka pot

Italy's love affair with coffee started with the moka pot – a cooker-top or electric coffee maker that brews by passing boiled water pressurised by steam through ground coffee. The moka pot was first invented for a world trade show in Milan in 1906, and went through various designs until an engineer called Alfonso Bialetti came up with a sleek version in 1933. It has hardly changed since, though it didn't become a household item until the 1950s, when Bialetti's sons decided to devote his shop to the sale of one item: the Bialetti Moka Express. It's estimated 90 per cent of the coffee in Italy is still drunk at home, and there's something beautiful about the ritual of filling a moka pot with freshly ground coffee and letting it simmer over the hob while you potter around the kitchen.

ILLUSTRATIONS: AMY LEONARD

Sicilian coffee granita

In the searing heat of Sicilian summers, iced coffee is taken one step further with granita – essentially shaved ice infused with bittersweet espresso, sometimes topped with cream. Recipes vary even between the different cities in Sicily, but granita is traditionally made with espresso, sugar and water, then frozen to a desired consistency. Traditionalists enjoy it for breakfast scooped on to a sweet brioche bun. It is also served on its own in a glass, with a dollop of whipped cream or your favourite liqueur drizzled on top.

The bicerin

Turin, in northern Italy, serves a delightfully decadent mix of chocolate, coffee and cream known as bicerin, which has long been warding off the chill of the city's cold winters and mountainous climes. Named after the bar where it was invented in 1763, these little mugs of bittersweet cosiness have become a symbol of the city. In the nearby city of Alessandria in Piedmont, a coffee-and-cocoa combination served in a glass is known as a marocchino. In Alba, home of Ferrero's chocolate industry, Nutella is used instead of cocoa powder.

Third-wave coffee

This movement takes the drink to an artisan level. The speciality coffee scene might have been championed in the US and Canada, but it has a rightful place in Italy. Coffee expert Helena Kyriakides runs private tastings and barista workshops in Bologna through her company Yummy Italy. She often introduces visitors to Bologna's third-wave coffee shops, such as Caffè Terzi, where beans are hand selected from all over the world. In Florence, hip baristas at Simbiosi Café serve up single-origin coffee to locals and visitors, while Australian-owned bistro and bakery Melaleuca overlooking the River Arno takes pride in its speciality coffee.

Words: **Phoebe Hunt**

Around the block

Why forcing yourself to keep going when the creative spark just won't come can lead to hurt and burnout

Creative frustration is the sound of a writer slamming their head into a keyboard, the sight of a performer frozen to the spot or the musty smell of dust-covered painting utensils. A common diagnosis for this proverbial brick wall is so-called block, its mention alone enough to evoke images of brain fog and a fundamental lack of knowing 'what next?'. Those who experience it often feel hurt, inadequate and helpless, and know that overcoming it will be challenging. Then there's the question of supposed treatment. Should you follow the advice of some sports coaches to simply 'walk it off' and push yourself to keep going? It's an option that will work for some, but in my experience, it led to a different issue – burnout.

Unlike block, burnout comes not from being unsure or unable to write, perform or paint (though it can be a side-effect), but from pressuring yourself to the point of fizzling out. For those artists who have no choice but to cram their creativity into the gaps between earning a living, nurturing relationships and looking after others (while achieving societal-imposed standards of perfection) it can be easy to give too much in the pursuit of artistic passion, dismissing tiredness as procrastination and feeling guilty about unused moments. It's often at these times that the inner sports coach starts yelling to 'suck it up and pick up the slack' even if that leads to disaster. However, an internalised belief that even the shortest period off is wasted can often do more harm than good.

The last time I permitted my inner sports coach to take control – I imagine him as a middle-aged former American footballer called Chuck with stern, unforgiving eyebrows – he really went to town on my mental health. Although I might have had more words in me, I lacked the motivation to put them to paper and, quite frankly, I couldn't think of anything worse. It took me months to get over Chuck's incessant demand that I continue, and most annoying was that all the warning signs had been there long before the feelings of disillusionment and self-doubt became all-consuming. Had I paused for a day or maybe even a few hours, it might have made a difference. It might even have prevented that single day of block from turning into the months of distress. Of course, not everyone has the privilege of dropping the tools of their trade at the early signs of burnout – deadlines often have to be met and bills have to be paid. So, what can be done when Chuck's heaping on the pressure, projects have to be filed and expectations have to be fulfilled, but the block won't shift?

Arguably, the first step is to recognise the problem – that your creativity is suffering from overexertion and could soon come to a crashing halt. The next stage can be trickier, especially for those with deadlines, as it involves finding an alternative to a complete full stop. You could ask yourself, however, if a project might be approached from a different angle or see if it's possible to harness creative frustrations and find an alternative, albeit temporary, home for them. A painter might turn to journalling, for example, or a performer might take time out for gardening. The idea is to explore or express those blocked passions in another artistic way. If circumstances allow, you might even negotiate an extended deadline (as I did for this article) to give yourself time to accommodate any feelings of impending burnout.

The truth is that burnout hurts and anyone who's been there knows the despondency and self-resentment that comes with it. From my experience, I would suggest that once you find yourself, creatively speaking, it's nigh impossible to lose yourself. But it is possible to forget what you've found when things get too much. During these times, remember as best as you can who you are as an artist and why it's important that you keep creating – it will keep you in tune with your imagination, ready to pick up the pen, the paintbrush or the mic when you're ready again. Be kind and patient, too, as caring for your mental health is paramount no matter the circumstances. Block doesn't last forever, but how you treat yourself during burnout can affect how you approach similar issues in the future. Give your inner sports coach a hug (Chuck appreciated his) and tell them it'll be all right in the end. Because it will.

Words: Alex Bowers

Wet and wild

Wetlands aren't just home to some of the world's most incredible wildlife, they're also vital sanctuaries for the soul

ANCIENT WATERS

The Everglades, US

Warm water spills over the top of my trainers as I follow my guide, Captain Steve, through drifting dawn mist and a tangle of ancient trees in the Big Cypress National Preserve, walking our way deeper into the wild. We've left the safety of Steve's elevated, all-terrain swamp buggy to explore this magical part of the US on foot and look for Mama: a two metre-long American alligator – one of an estimated 1.25 million that live in the state's waterways, along with around 2,000 American crocodiles.

Big Cypress borders the Everglades National Park: a Unesco World Heritage Site, International Biosphere Reserve and Wetland of International Importance, covering 1.5 million acres of southern Florida. The Park was established in 1947, but the larger Everglades ecosystem dates back 5,000 years and springs from the Kissimmee River, which runs into Lake Okeechobee, with waters from the lake slowly flowing south to the Florida Bay.

This vast subtropical wilderness is stitched from a patchwork of landscapes including sawgrass prairies, hardwood hammocks, pinelands, mangrove swamps and coastal lowlands, where bobcats, black bears and elusive Florida panthers roam. For thousands of years, it has also been home to Native American groups, with many Seminole and Miccosukee people still living in the region today.

The Everglades supports almost 800 kinds of native seed-bearing plants and 360 types of bird, including the red-shouldered hawk and swallow-tailed kite, along with more than 20 species of snake, including four that are venomous – the Florida cottonmouth, eastern diamondback rattlesnake, dusky pygmy rattlesnake and eastern coral snake. A fifth-generation Gladesman, Captain Steve's knee-high, reinforced camouflage snake boots clearly aren't just for show – if only I'd thought to pack mine...

Hiking trails and boardwalks allow a glimpse into the Everglades' primordial landscape, where bromeliads and Spanish moss cling to cypress trees, rare white ghost orchids light up the shadows, and armoured reptiles from a prehistoric age wallow in its pools. But taking a leap of faith with Captain Steve and leaving the well-trodden paths behind offers me a unique opportunity to sense as well as see this extraordinary landscape and observe its incredible creatures, while the same waters that sustain them soak my feet.

When we locate Mama, after 30 minutes of wading through sodden grasses, roots and shoots, she is submerged in classic

'For most of history, man has had to fight nature to survive; in this century he is beginning to realise that in order to survive, he must protect it'

JACQUES COUSTEAU

gator style, motionless with her snout and eyes above the waterline, seeing all but undisturbed by our presence. Finding her here in her steamy swampland home prompts a sharp intake of breath. She is magnificent: an apex predator swirling out of the mists of time, snapping me out of my comfort zone.

Beyond the protective boundary of the national park, airboats provide a drier and speedier way to explore the Everglades, venturing into areas that are inaccessible on foot, but while the alligators seem unfazed as the boats roar across the 'river of grass', herons and rare wood storks take flight. Visitors are given ear protectors; the resident wildlife isn't so lucky.

For a more tranquil experience, I take a guided kayak trip to the Ten Thousand Islands National Wildlife Refuge – a chain of untouched isles supporting rich estuarine, mangrove and marsh habitat. Here, the turquoise waters of the Gulf of Mexico provide a playground for bottle-nosed dolphins, Florida manatees and turtles, which nest on the islands from May to September. Combing the shallows of the sun-drenched shoreline we see conches, lightning whelks, horseshoe crabs and rays, while ospreys and brown pelicans soar overhead.

'The Everglades is alive with wildlife,' Captain Steve whispers, as we watch Mama back in Big Cypress, the heat of the Florida day rising around us. 'It gets beneath people's skin – it's very special.' He speaks the truth. As I leave this ancient wilderness behind, its raw beauty and gently flowing waters stay with me: they stay with me still.

For more on the Everglades, visit paradisecoast.co.uk and visitflorida.com. Information about Captain Steve and kayak tours can be found at captainstevesswampbuggyadventures.com and evergladesareatours.com respectively.

See travel.state.gov for the latest advice on restrictions.

Turn over to explore more wonderful wetlands

MAP OF DREAMS

East Anglia, UK

I climb down the steps from the pontoon and swim out into Fritton Lake, before rolling onto my back, closing my eyes and offering my face to the warm sun. As the nutrient-rich water buoys my body, I notice my tightened jaw softening, hunched shoulders starting to drop, and even a brow furrowed with frustration and fatigue beginning to unknot. Floating under a weeping willow, which softly rustles and rains a shower of leaves from above, my worries hitch a ride on the cobalt-blue dragonflies whirring around me and are swiftly carried away.

Fresh water supports a diverse array of life on Earth, but we're learning that it sustains our spirit and protects our mental health, too. New research, released by the UK's Mental Health Foundation (MHF) reveals that 65 per cent of people find that being near water improves their wellbeing and that it's their favourite thing about being in nature. Over the summer, a new Blue Prescribing project from the MHF and Wildfowl & Wetlands Trust offered people experiencing poor mental health who lacked access to water in natural settings the chance to join a six-week nature-driven health programme at the London Wetland Centre – a wild and watery oasis in the capital.

Here at Fritton Lake, a members' holiday club on the Norfolk/Suffolk border, the waters don't take long to weave their healing magic. Close to the rivers and marshlands of the Norfolk Broads, Britain's largest nationally protected wetland, the club is set amid 1,000 acres of ancient woodlands, wildflowers and fields on the Somerleyton Estate. But the estate's two-mile forest-fringed lake keeps pulling me back: to paddle board, to swim, to sit and dream, and even to sweat. Fritton's Koto sauna is one of a floating kind, bobbing on a tree-shaded pontoon with a panoramic view of the lake. If you're lucky, you'll catch sight of the estate's free-roaming red and fallow deer, Exmoor ponies, Highland cattle, pigs or four resident Asian water buffalo, basking on the opposite bank, as you steam away your worries.

The astonishing beauty of Fritton is part of a wider – and wilder – picture: a bold, brave mission to return 250,000 acres of East Anglia back to nature. WildEast is the vision of three local landowners and businessmen, including Hugh Crossley or Lord Somerleyton, who lives with his family on the estate. 'Over the past four years, Fritton's farmlands have gradually been restored to carefully managed and sustainable wild land, which supports a diverse number of plant and animal species,' explains Hugh. 'The WildEast conservation project is not just restoring habitats and preserving wildlife. It's also reconnecting people with nature and inspiring them to share our vision.' Unlike

'Man's heart away from nature becomes hard'

STANDING BEAR

some of the world's other significant wetland areas, East Anglia is highly populated, with several cities including Norwich and Peterborough. Just a few hours from London, the region was one of the kingdoms of Anglo-Saxon England, and has been settled for thousands of years. Historically, it was a centre for wool, but agriculture remains economically important, with barley the region's most prolific crop.

Rivers wind through the towns, flowing onwards into The Wash or the North Sea. The Norfolk Broads – known as the Venice of the East – has around 40 inland broads and over 125 miles of navigable lock-free waterways: more than either the Italian city or Amsterdam. For many years they were thought to have evolved naturally, but in the 1950s botanist Joyce Lambert discovered they'd been formed by the extraction of peat, used for fuel and construction. By the 14th century,

the flooded channels had become a haven for wildlife and later, a vital means of transportation, with unique Norfolk wherry sailing boats ferrying cargo and people from the 1600s, and recreational cruisers becoming popular in the 1930s. These days, the Broads attract eight million visitors a year, who enjoy boating, birdwatching and exploring the region's villages.

'East Anglia is home to some of the UK's most important wetlands and many associated rare and iconic species,' says University College London's Carl Sayer, a wetlands expert and member of WildEast. 'But all is not well.' Across the UK, biodiversity is in drastic decline, with once-common species now teetering on the brink of extinction. 'Ecological restoration is needed urgently,' says Carl. 'A nature recovery is possible, but we must think big and act decisively.' WildEast's interactive Map of Dreams ticks both these critical boxes. Launched in early 2021, it encourages people to make a pledge to restore nature in any way that they can. Whether that's farmers replanting lost hedgerows to provide wildlife habitat, landowners resurrecting long-lost ponds to attract rare amphibians like newts, or gardeners choosing to go pesticide-free, everyone who makes a pledge becomes a WildEast stakeholder, with the chance of benefitting from the project's sustainable growth over the next 50 years. The goal is to have one million pledges by 2025. 'We've been overwhelmed by the response,' says Hugh. 'Adults and children have offered time, land, money, experience, sweat and tears to help restore what's been lost and protect what we still have. Nature is resilient and ready to flourish when it's given a fair and lasting chance, and in our region, WildEast is that chance.'

Before leaving Fritton Lake, I join foraging and wildlife guru Matthew Stevenson for a ramble around the grounds, tasting herbs and edible flowers as we go. These home-grown treats are used by Fritton's chefs in their seasonal menus, along with fruit and veg from the estate and ingredients from small local producers. Jumping on to The Bittern, Fritton Lake's motorised launch, we cruise the length of the waterway by launch, passing cormorants dipping for fish, while elegant grey herons watch us beadily from the banks. The ancient trees of the wild woods soar from the shore into a cloudless blue sky, lifting my spirits with them. WildEast might be creating a Map of Dreams, but here, those dreams have already become an exciting reality.

Learn more about Fritton Lake at frittonlake.co.uk and WildEast at wildeast.co.uk. Explore the Broads at visitnorfolk.co.uk.

Visit gov.uk for the latest advice on restrictions.

ON TOP DOWN UNDER

Kakadu National Park, Australia

'The traditional landowners' relationship to "country" is very strong,' says my Venture North Safaris guide Dave McMahon, as we walk a sandy trail lined with pandanus trees to a secluded waterhole for a cooling escape from the heat of the day. 'Country takes in all aspects of the landscape, and the local people have custodial responsibility to look after everything that lives within it.'

Just three hours drive east from Darwin, the tropical capital of Australia's Northern Territory, lies Kakadu National Park. A Unesco World Heritage Site – listed for both its natural and cultural significance – its geological history dates back billions of years, and Aboriginal people have lived here for more than 65,000 years. Covering around 7,700 square miles, Kakadu is home to pristine wetlands, lush rainforests, waterfalls plunging into crystal pools, and uniquely Australian wildlife, including wallabies, sugar gliders and dingoes.

Soaring escarpments conceal ancient galleries of some of the oldest surviving rock art: 20,000-year-old stories painted in

'Study nature, love nature, stay close to nature. It will never fail you'

FRANK LLOYD WRIGHT

PHOTOGRAPHS: TOURISM NORTHERN TERRITORY

hematite and ochre, shining a light on the lives of the region's custodians – the Bininj and Mungguy – and the native animals that share their land. Also pictured are ancestral creation beings that Aboriginal people believe shaped their country during the Dreamtime, including the Lightning Man, Namarrgon. Painted at Kakadu's Burrunggui, or Nourlangie Rock, this powerful being reappears each year, heralding the arrival of tropical summer storms. The Rainbow Serpent, known as Almudj or Bolung, can be seen at the rock art site of Ubirr, honouring her role in forming the land's waterholes, supporting the lifecycles of its animals and plants.

Sadly, in common with other wetlands, the national park is at risk from the impacts of climate change, human activity and invasive species. A strategy has been in place since 2014 to maintain Kakadu's biodiversity, improve fire management, control fishing and support the recovery of threatened plant and animal species, with Aboriginal custodians playing a key role in the programme. Seeing the sunset sky burn purple over Nourlangie as cockatoos swoop down to rest, watching flocks of hundreds of magpie geese fill the skies over the floodplains, or taking a sunrise cruise on the Yellow Water Billabong (Ngurrungurrudjba) as boat-long crocodiles languidly patrol the banks, it's clear that Kakadu's nature game remains strong.

Hot and humid, the region's summer monsoon season, known as 'The Wet', sees tropical rains and storms fill Kakadu's plains, rivers and water holes, as the park floods with even more life. Water lilies carpet the billabongs, while thousands of water birds flock to the wetlands and the park's waterfalls display their full, thundering glory. This spectacular land has supported an abundance of plants and wildlife for millennia, sustaining the country's traditional custodians in a safe and spiritual home: long may their sacred natural sanctuary stand.

Discover more about Kakadu National Park at parksaustralia. gov.au/kakadu and northernterritory.com. For information on adventure safaris in Australia's Northern Territory, visit venturenorth.com.au

See australia.gov.au for the latest advice on quarantine restrictions.

Words: **Lauren Jarvis**
Lauren is a travel writer with a special interest in wildlife, wellness, adventure and conservation. See @laurenjarvistravels

All holiday areas are asking travellers to be responsible and follow their own and their destination country's up-to-date information.

MINDFULNESS

'You have to go the way your blood beats. If you don't live the only life you
have, you won't live some other life, you won't live any life at all'

James Baldwin

On body and soul

How to feel more at home in your physical being

Have you ever caught a glimpse of your reflection and noticed the difficult emotion you'd been struggling with written all over your face? So much of what goes on in your body is a mystery. In the same vein, I've often started a yoga practice only to discover a profound tightness I had no idea was there, or pain and tension I'd been holding in my body without being aware of it.

The truth is, many people spend vast amounts of time lost in thought, worrying about the future or ruminating on a story from their past. But what if we paid more attention to what's going on inside ourselves in the here and now – and the way our thoughts and feelings were being played out in our bodies? It sounds obvious, but it's surprisingly easy to forget that everything begins and ends in the body – that is experiences, the things seen, the people interacted with, the emotions felt and the thoughts had.

Our body is our means to being in the world – and it's the reason we literally carry around the difficult experiences we've had. To use an expression often quoted in relation to the body-oriented therapy Somatic Experiencing, 'the issue is in our tissues'. It's no wonder then that we view our physical self as the sum of who we are. Yet this is only part of the picture. Because, while every body is a manifestation of the physical and emotional experiences it's had – from the springy energy of a young child to the slumped shoulders of someone experiencing depression – this is only one aspect of what it means to be human.

Ultimately, our physical bodies offer a gateway to our inner life, the truest part of us, according to author and spiritual teacher Eckhart Tolle, where the 'joy of being emanates'. He believes many people are detached from the essence of who they are, a state of being he calls 'inner spaciousness', which goes beyond mind or personality. In his book *A New Earth*, Eckhart

writes of the formless self that transcends the body after death as both who you really are and the energy field of your body. But how do you reach this part of yourself? The first step is by learning how to be present in your body, and acknowledging the physical impact that your emotions have on you. Everyone has a window of tolerance but life can push you out of your range of optimal functioning. To thrive, you need to learn how to put yourself back together again. If you don't, and instead avoid difficult feelings and physical sensations, you can increase the chance of feeling overwhelmed by them.

Somantic stress

In *Burnout: The Secret to Unlocking the Stress Cycle*, researchers Emily and Amelia Nagoski examine what happens in the body when the limbic system – known as the emotional brain – is constantly activated and gets stuck in the fight, flight or freeze mode. They break this down into a series of steps that begin with a stressor, an event or situation that occurs in the external world, such as sitting in heavy traffic on the way to work every day or constantly having to be polite to a difficult colleague. This turns into stress – the physical symptoms felt in the body, such as an increased heart rate, tense shoulders and shallow breathing, and can lead to more pervasive symptoms such as sleep disturbances and digestive issues.

The crucial part, they say, involves giving the body the resources it needs to complete the stress cycles that get activated every day. This could include any physical activity you enjoy, such as walking, running or swimming, or even just tensing all of your muscles before releasing them while sitting at your desk. 'Remember, your body has no idea what "filing your taxes" or "resolving an interpersonal conflict" means,' they write. 'Speak its language, [which] is body language.' But what

happens when you don't manage to complete the stress cycle and those difficult experiences and feelings stay with you?

According to somatic movement specialist and yoga therapist Aimée Tañón, by fostering a strong mind-body connection, you can learn how to be more resilient when difficult, and often deeply held, feelings arise. 'The fact is there's a strong link between difficult physical sensations and difficult emotions or feelings,' she explains. 'During my classes, we'll go into a pose and often it might feel tense – there may be some stiffness or mild pain there – and this often triggers the memory of a story or difficult event from the past. That's because these events are actually buried deep in our tissues.' The important thing, Aimée asserts, is to learn how to feel this, to stay with it and then let it go. 'When we learn to breathe through the discomfort and feel the sensation of our muscles releasing, we develop self-knowledge and become empathetic with ourselves.'

Taking this form of interior knowledge or intelligence further, psychiatrist Bessel van der Kolk describes the process of interoception as an 'awareness of our subtle sensory, body-based feelings' in his book *The Body Keeps the Score*. Rather than completing the daily stress cycle or meeting difficult sensations on the yoga mat, interoception is a process that enables an individual to stay calm and take control before a stressor can make an impact by learning to take a more objective view of the situation. In doing so, it's possible to override the emotional brain, instead activating the medial prefrontal cortex, the part of the brain responsible for choice-making.

It's no surprise then, that one of the best ways to cultivate interoception is through a mindfulness practice. In a recent talk on the fear of ageing and loss, meditation teacher, psychologist and author Tara Brach describes a state of bodily awareness that transcends stressors by going to the heart of difficult emotions, and feeling their shape, texture and even temperature. 'When we worry about what's ahead, how our body is going to change – whether we're afraid of turning 30 because we fear a decline in physical attractiveness or an increase in responsibility, or we're afraid of turning 75 and fear losing control of ourselves and becoming more dependent on others, we tighten our bodies,' she says. Notice the way anxiety feels in your body, and how you're being pulled into a story, by anchoring yourself in the present moment, she says. 'Pause for a moment and ask, what is this situation trying to teach me?'

Of course, it can take courage to do this, especially as paying attention is the opposite of distraction – an operating mode that can be at play in many people's lives. But it's something that, according to Buddhist nun, author and speaker Pema Chödrön, we're more likely to achieve if we can learn to come from a place of kindness and self-acceptance, and engage in a process that calls us to be present. Tara agrees: 'Only then can we develop intimacy with our inner life and each other. Only then can we connect to our inner beings – that transcend our bodies – and remember our belonging to spirit.'

Words: **Yvonne Gavan**

HOW TO FOSTER A STRONG MIND-BODY-SPIRIT CONNECTION

Ground

According to holistic health therapist Kate Edwards, noticing how your body makes contact with a surface, in a practice known as grounding, is a great way to foster bodily awareness.

'Find a comfortable position, either sitting upright in a chair or on the floor,' she says. 'Notice the sensation of your feet making contact with the earth, pressing down through the heel. Or the feeling of your legs on the floor where you're sitting. And feel that sensation of being held – in your seat or by the ground, feeling supported.

'Now notice your breathing, and the feeling of your muscles. Notice any places that feel more relaxed, or neutral. Focus on the softness and expansiveness in your body.'

Greet

While practising grounding, you might start to notice tension in the body accompanied by difficult thoughts and feelings.

'Try to meet the edge of that emotion and soften – allowing yourself to feel vulnerable,' advises, describing a process where difficult emotions are greeted, and given form before being lovingly released.

'Feel the knot and the heat, the "daggered" feeling in your chest. Allow yourself to sit with it until it's no longer uncomfortable. At first you're allowing the feeling – and then you're making friends with it.

'This is when you feel the heart breaking open. When you do this you'll come to a vast tender space. It's a place of belonging that lets us know all is well.'

Complete

Journalling is, according to Kate, one of the best ways to 'drop into the body' and complete a grounding and greeting practice.

'Start by describing how you're feeling in that moment. Remember you are writing for yourself, so use the pen to record any combination of words or images that come to mind – however unusual they may seem,' she says.

'Try to focus on your body. Are there any tight areas still? Where did you feel pain in the grounding practice? You might come up with descriptive words, like hot, heavy, sticky or jagged, or an image.

'If you managed to release that difficult emotion in the practice, how did it feel? Again, allow any descriptions or images to come to mind.

'Finally ask your body a question: is there anything else I need to do to complete this practice? Note the answer you get without judging or altering it in any way.'

Curb the chaos

*Chaotic thinking can bring inspired ideas but also lead to confusion
and a strong sense of being overwhelmed. There are, however, ways
that can help to moderate the negatives of a mind under stress*

If you've ever felt your mind was brimming over with random
thoughts, like an Instagram feed that's scrolling too fast for your
eyes to focus on anything, you might have been experiencing
chaotic thinking. Sometimes this hectic flash of ideas can bring
creative inspiration or cause a switch into superpower mode,
but if you feel you're in a battle with your own brain, especially
when those thoughts come thick and fast, it can be stressful too.
Here, US-based marriage and family therapist Elizabeth Hinkle
explains chaotic thinking and shares her guidance on how to
help curb the confusion it can bring.

What is chaotic thinking?

'It describes types of thoughts that flood your brain very quickly.
They can feel intense and overwhelming, and they don't always
make sense. These chaotic thoughts usually feel disorganised,
out of place and impulsive.'

What's the difference between chaotic and manic thinking?

'Chaos and mania are different beasts that manifest in various
ways. Chaos would typically be how you're responding to
a particular stressful situation. For example, you might be

clashing with a partner, which could lead to a barrage of thoughts like: "I can't take this any more" or "I don't know what to do" and "Why do we fight so much?"

'A manic episode comes from a chemical/biological response in the brain and isn't usually triggered by an outside event. It often includes irrational thoughts or ones that inflate reality, for example, thinking something like: "Nothing could hurt me right now, I am invincible." In extreme cases, mania involves impulsive and/or risk-taking behaviour that's out of character for that person.'

What makes a chaotic episode worse?
'Stress can make any type of thinking more chaotic and difficult. When we're stressed, we tend not to breathe as slowly or deeply. This can lead to reduced oxygen levels, which makes it harder to think clearly. It also creates anxious feelings that interfere with thought clarity and focus. Both chaotic and manic episodes could happen regardless of lifestyle choices or personality traits. However, a habit such as substance misuse could contribute to triggering or worsening an episode.'

Is feeling this way always negative, or can it be put to good use?
'It's rare that something happening is either solely good or bad. It seems much of this is about each person and what works for them. If your thoughts are bothering you, it's good to reach out and talk to a trusted family member or a friend and/or a professional when that's needed. If your thoughts help you to be more creative and it doesn't feel harmful, though, that's great.'

What types of therapy can help to calm chaotic thinking?
According to Talkspace, an online therapy website to which Elizabeth contributes, there are more than 50 types of therapeutic approaches, but some focus specifically on how people think. 'Cognitive behavioural therapy is the main one [see issue 30]. It helps people recognise those automatic and distorted types of thoughts, such as assumptions, and encourages them to think differently to encourage a different emotion.

'If, for example, someone hasn't responded to your text and the thought "they must hate me" crosses your mind, it's helpful

to focus on the facts. [You could think] something like: "I don't know why she hasn't replied. She could be busy right now. It might not have anything to do with me." Usually a person will feel less upset if they practise techniques like this.'

When should you ask for help?
'If you notice thoughts are disturbing you on a regular basis, it could be a sign it's a good time to seek professional help. Reach out immediately if you are having thoughts of hurting yourself or someone else.'

Words: Claire Blackmore

HOW TO MOVE PAST DIFFICULT THINKING TO A CALMER PLACE

1. **Identify**. Work out how you're feeling and clarify the emotion you're experiencing. Is it sadness, anger, hurt, confusion?

2. **Understand**. Unpick what has contributed to your feeling this way and any potential triggers that might have been responsible for it.

3. **Recognise**. Once you're aware of how you feel and why, look again at your emotions. As Elizabeth emphasises, feelings aren't right or wrong, good or bad, they are what they are. You aren't agreeing or disagreeing with the emotion, you are recognising it.

4. **Reframe**. Remind yourself that emotions come and go. Stick to the facts and find a mantra you find calming. Try reframing your thoughts to ones that are more helpful to you – and seek professional help with this if needed.

ILLUSTRATIONS: MAGDA AZAB

SLOW IT DOWN

Active ways to help tame chaotic thoughts

- **Take deep, slow breaths**. Inhale through your nose and out through your mouth for a few minutes to improve oxygen intake.
- **Move your body**. Walking, stretching, yoga, jogging, or even just dancing around your kitchen, could help.
- **Check your fluid intake and nutrition**. The NHS Eatwell Guide (nhs.uk) recommends drinking six to eight glasses of fluid daily – besides water, lower-fat milk, tea and coffee count – and having at least five portions of a variety of fruit and veg a day. Also make sure you're eating at regular intervals.
- **Put pen to paper**. Write down your chaotic thoughts if you can, as it might help to process them later.
- **Open up**. Talk to a friend or a family member, or reach out for help from a professional therapist.

If you're experiencing a mental health crisis and need immediate help, the following organisations all offer free and confidential advice and support 24/7: samaritans.org, giveusashout.org, crisistextline.org.
For more of Elizabeth's thoughts, visit talkspace.com. You can also find Talkspace on Facebook, Instagram and Twitter @Talkspace.

Happiness hazard

Why telling a loved one you 'only want them to be happy' isn't always the best policy

Ever said something with the best possible intentions only to have it completely misread and take a torrid turn? Most of us have, so reach for the sentence we think will make it all better: 'I just want you to be happy.' Only it doesn't.

The words are intended to be helpful, the idea being to relieve someone you care about of any other burdens or expectations they imagine you might have of them. It seems a simple and supportive statement, but to the person on the receiving end, that's often not the case. 'To say, "just be happy" indicates that negative emotions are not accepted,' explains Jennifer Cawley, psychotherapist at The School of Life, a London-based organisation offering books, seminars and online classes designed to help find calm, self-understanding, resilience and connection. 'Instead, we must allow those we love to feel the full spectrum of emotions and encourage them to feel safe experiencing all of them. As soon as we label emotions good and bad, we are taking away natural human experiences, which can cause further confusion down the line.'

Often, the request to just be happy comes at a time of stress or hardship. A person might be miserable at work, struggling in a relationship or confused as to which life path to follow. Whatever the circumstance, rather than being reassuring, it can have the opposite effect. In the face of confusion or indecision, small certitudes can manifest as much bigger obstacles and expressing any definite emotion can be hard. What if someone doesn't know how to be happy? What if they can't find the thing that makes them happy? It's easy to see how being unable to achieve what is presented as a simple task could make someone feel as though they've failed.

But happy isn't a binary concept. 'The search for happiness can also be a way to find meaning in life – if we've hit upon happiness, we've perhaps found meaning, albeit momentarily,' says Jennifer. 'However, it's often [found] from having navigated through difficult times and accessing inner resources that we might otherwise never have known we had. That in itself is confidence-building.' So, joy is easier to locate once a crisis has passed, which means suggesting to someone in the middle of a crunch situation that they be happy is likely to be unhelpful and impossible for them to achieve.

For many, the phrase 'I just want you to be happy' is part and parcel of their teenage years. It's a heartfelt and genuine message said by guardians the world over as they try to guide their children through the combined assault of raging hormones, schoolwork, and friendship and relationship traumas. But child psychologists are now suggesting it's not the positive advice many believe it to be. 'Within it, there's an implicit message of: "If you're not happy, there is something wrong with you,"' says Jennifer. Yet the reality is that finding reliable feelings of happiness in adolescence is slim. Fortunately, the discussion of mental wellbeing has progressed in recent years and feelings of sadness are now widely considered to be part of a healthy emotional balance. This can be tough to observe as a loved one but it's an important process to be a part of, be that from the perspective of parent, child, partner or friend. It's easy to feel the best approach is to fix things, to make everything better, take the strain, lighten the mood and lift the spirits. But emotions of disappointment, failure and regret can be healing, so it can be helpful to find different ways to explore what someone is experiencing (see below).

In truth, when you're at your lowest, finding happiness is about as easy as retrieving a lost contact lens on the beach, and when you do fall upon moments of bliss, they're fleeting. That's the nature of this emotion – it comes and goes, ebbs and flows. So, when someone close is in a difficult place, try not to push away their sadness, worries or anxiety while presenting them with an unachievable single target of happiness. Respecting their emotions and reassuring them of your patience, love and understanding might prove to be more encouraging words.

ALTERNATIVE OPTIONS

Rather than use the imperative to just be happy, here are a few different phrases that might be helpful:

- *I'm here with you, no matter how you feel so let's just sit with this, shall we?*
- *What is it that sparks your interest right now, even in the tiniest way?*
- *Small wins will make today a success, so let's just focus on that.*

Words: **Jess Lacey**

BE
HAPPY

Beneath the hurt

At the darkest of times, forgiveness has the power to let in a glimmer of light

Forgiveness is a process that might sound good in theory but can be difficult to put into practice, especially when it comes to pardoning people who've caused you great pain. It's often hard to know where to begin. American psychologist and retired professor Everett Worthington has devoted much of his research career and clinical practice to teaching people how to forgive. For him, the topic is deeply personal. Decades ago, he chose to forgive the person who killed his mother (see overleaf). According to Everett, for some people part of what makes it tempting to hold on to a grudge is they enjoy feeling resentful. 'It makes them feel more powerful to be angry at someone, and maybe motivated to get back at the person.' He compares it to overeating or staying up too late – people know it's not a good idea, but in the moment it feels good.

Health effects

Yet like overeating or neglecting sleep, holding a grudge can have adverse effects on your health. It turns out the old saying 'holding a grudge is like drinking poison and expecting the other person to get sick' bears some truth. Evidence-based studies have shown that your state of mind can affect you physically, in positive or negative ways. Carrying resentment can act like a pressure on the system, activating the body's stress response, which unleashes cortisol into the bloodstream. Chronically elevated cortisol levels can increase the risk

of having a heart attack and stroke, and interfere with the immune system. On the flip side, the act of forgiveness can be beneficial. Research has shown a connection between it and higher levels of happiness, fewer symptoms of anxiety and depression and lower pain levels for those with a chronic condition. A recent study found a connection between self-forgiveness and slower cognitive decline in older people.

Another researcher, Loren Toussaint, professor of psychology at Luther College in the US, believes that forgiveness is 'related to longer life in general, so you tend to die later of all causes'. He advises anyone struggling to 'know you're not alone'. He adds: 'For a lot of people forgiveness does not come easily. There are also instances where it seems to come very quickly, even for very significant things, but that's not the norm.'

According to both researchers it can be helpful to make a distinction between forgiveness and reconciliation. People can assume that the former means letting the person who hurt you back into your life. However, says Everett, 'forgiveness is really independent of reconciling'. Loren sees it as an internal process that involves transforming thoughts, emotions, feelings and motivations from negative to neutral, or even positive. He says he's often asked if survivors of abuse should forgive the perpetrators: 'I say, it's entirely up to the victim whether or not they want to forgive an abuser. But I would not recommend reconciling with them, because if someone has hurt you in the

past, there's a good probability they might do so again in the future. I don't want to encourage people to go back to places of vulnerability or ones where they might be harmed again.'

Personal process

Another misconception is that forgiveness means letting the offender off the hook. Everett stresses this is not the case, in his opinion, if his mother's killer were to be caught 'the fact that I've forgiven him would make no difference – he would still have to face justice in exactly the same way'. Loren says that at the outset of the forgiveness process, it's helpful to be clear with yourself about what the original offence was and what you want from the situation. 'Is it something in particular that you'll forgive them for? Or have they just been a horrible person all your life and you want to try to forgive them for being who they are? Those are different things – and obviously a very different kind of process will have to unfold.'

The next step is trying to empathise with, or humanise, the offender. Key to this is remembering that you might have wronged others too. 'People hurt us, and we're offended, and we don't want to forgive them,' Loren says. 'But we also hurt other people and offend them, and we want their forgiveness.' He says

a key turning point comes 'when you can realise you simply cannot get through life productively with hatred in your heart, especially if it comes to dominate your perspective and your feelings on a day-to-day basis'. He adds: 'You have to find some way to take the evil out of the wrongdoer, in your eyes, and understand them as a human being, just like you, deserving of the same things that you hope you might deserve some day.'

In an essay titled *Why I Forgave*, Steven McDonald, a New York City police officer who was shot and paralysed, expresses a similar sentiment. He writes: 'I believe the only thing worse than receiving a bullet in my spine would have been to nurture revenge in my heart.' In some cases, forgiveness can also mean letting go of the search for answers. Sometimes the offender's motives aren't clear. 'We call something "senseless violence" for a reason – it's senseless,' says Loren. 'There is no logic… So there's got to be an end to a search for understanding or meaning in a situation where there might not be one.' Forgiveness is ultimately a gift you can give yourself. It doesn't mean forgetting what's been done to you, but rather allowing yourself the freedom to move on.

Words: Jillian Bell

FORGIVING THE UNTHINKABLE

Everett began researching forgiveness in 1990. Little did he know his research would be put to a cruel test six years later, when his mother was murdered by a burglar. Police believe the person broke into her house thinking it was empty, and killed her when she confronted them.

Everett's initial reaction was one of shock and anger. He remembers sitting in his brother's room with his siblings the following night and gazing at a baseball bat leaning against the wall. He told them: 'I wish whoever did that was here. I would take that baseball bat and beat his brains out.'

Unable to fall asleep that night, he began working on his mother's eulogy. As he thought about her and her life, he says that 'it just came to me that here I am, a researcher in forgiveness... and yet I had gone almost 24 hours and never allowed that word to enter my mind'.

He began to imagine his mother's killer as a young teen who'd been overtaken by anger and fear when their perfect crime was spoiled, and he recalled his own anger earlier that evening. 'I thought, wait a minute – whose heart is darker here? This kid with the impulse-control problem, who's afraid, and angry – or me, this mature man?' He realised that if he could be forgiven for his own rage, so, too, could his mother's killer. He committed then and there to forgive them.

Model for forgiveness

Everett has developed a formula for forgiveness that he calls the REACH model. It's the same process he worked through when he forgave his mother's murderer, and it's been proven to be effective in more than 30 randomised control trials around the world. Here's the formula:

R is for recall: try to remember the hurtful event as objectively as you can.
E is for empathise: try to see the perspective of the person who hurt you.
A is for altruism: remember a time when you hurt someone else and you were forgiven. Next, offer that same unearned gift of forgiveness to the person who hurt you.
C is for committing: commit to publicly forgiving the person who wronged you.
H is for hold on: remember the choice you've made to forgive. This doesn't mean forgetting or ignoring the hurt.

If you're using this model, or trying to forgive someone, these questions could help get you started:

- What is it costing me to hold this grudge? Could I try letting go of these negative emotions for the sake of my own wellbeing?
- What would justice look like in this situation? How might forgiving this person be possible, even if justice is not served?
- Do I want to reconcile with this person? What changes would I need to see them make in order to do so?
- Have there been times when I've hurt someone and been forgiven? How can I show the same grace to the person who's wounded me?

Matters of choice

Some make them breezily in seconds, others agonise for days, but bringing conscious awareness to the decisions you make can help you to plan and build a fulfilling future

In life, outcomes, energies and emotions are all affected by the choices you make. Some are day to day, such as: 'Should I take the bus or drive?' Others are more important and potentially life-changing. Certain situations might hold out the promise of excitement, but you choose not to go there because it's not the right time or place for them, or they might have to stay on the back-burner because of physical, emotional or financial constraints. When faced with an important decision, opting for one choice over another will, naturally, produce different consequences. What those outcomes would otherwise have been can only be guessed at. Reflecting on this aspect of reality back in 1915, the American poet Robert Frost wrote: 'Two roads diverged in a wood and I took the one less travelled by. And that has made all the difference.'

True to say, choice can be a force for good. It can boost confidence and give clarity and courage to step forward, while the freedom to exert your will can feel like an incredible strength. When you become more conscious of the choices that exist, on an everyday level and in more unusual circumstances, you can focus on how to select what works best for you. There will, of course, be times when the outcome isn't what you expected or were hoping for, but this can also bring greater awareness of what you want more (and less) of in your life. And being aware of these factors can help shape future decisions.

What is being consciously chosen, and how?

Feelings exert a greater or lesser influence on how decisions are approached. In that respect, the same situation could seem as easy as opening a packet of crisps or as challenging as climbing Mount Everest, depending on the day, time and a person's level of vulnerability in any given moment. With this in mind, try to step outside any negative feelings and view each situation from a neutral standpoint. Most people are more capable of making decisions than they give themselves credit for. It could also be that there are more options available than might seem immediately apparent. This isn't to suggest that switching viewpoint will make decision-making easy or straightforward. There are times when a person's influence is limited and someone else will get to choose how to proceed. The outcome might not be what they wanted, or in their best interests, but they know in their heart that's what they'll have to do, if only for now.

At other times it might be necessary to say no to a person or opportunity – even one that was previously desired – because the reality of the situation no longer meets expectations or it feels like the most appropriate decision for everyone concerned. Even here, though, there can be a positive side. Saying no, in fact, can give a person clarity and focus about what's important to them. It's a statement that shows they have explicit boundaries. And while it might not always be easy to say no, it can be viewed as an assured and purposeful choice.

Where will it lead?

In some ways, the direction a person takes can be less important than the fact they're opening doors to possibility. To evolve, it's necessary to move forward and change, often developing greater resilience, fortitude and prowess in the process. And these traits can help to lay the foundations for dreams, visions and goals to come true.

Mindful choosing and decision-making can bring fresh perspectives and the ability to make the positive changes necessary for personal development. It can provide the strength to break self-limiting habits and the tenacity to stick to commitments. The road to transformation awaits.

Words: **Bhavya Arora**
Bhavya is a certified coach and runs workshops teaching people how to reach their potential. Find out more at forwardfocuslondon.com.

Turn the page to discover some of Bhavya's decision-making tips

HOW TO MAKE
EFFECTIVE CHOICES

- Do not live in fear of the need to make the perfect decision.

- There is no right or wrong, it's all a learning process.

- Face, notice and acknowledge all options with courage.

- Try to approach a situation with confidence, even if you have reservations about it.

- Weigh up your possibilities and go with the ones that are best for you.

- Once you've made a decision, own it and think carefully before asking for validation from others.

- Be brave about your choices, as you've nothing to prove or feel guilty about.

...and factors to consider

- Faced with a choice, listen carefully and take your time. This applies to verbal and non-verbal situations.

- You don't have to jump in and make snap decisions. Step back and review. Pay attention to the details.

- Don't act when controlled by your inner critic, emotions of anger, frustration or fear, or if you're feeling exploited or deceived.

- Shift perspectives. Try to view the situation as though you were an impartial observer and see how things might be done differently.

- If your decision will affect others, consider and value their viewpoint, too.

- Don't start with 'I can't do it' – tell yourself you'll give it a go. It's okay if the outcome isn't what you wished for, at least you'll have tried.

- Don't be scared of making mistakes. Learning from what seemed to go wrong is the key to success.

- Recall options you'd previously considered. Can they be useful now?

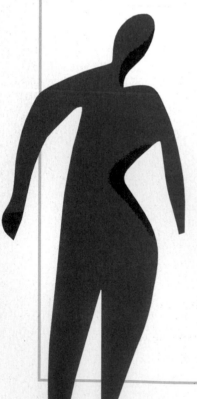

Moments of trust

It can take years to build and be shattered in an instant, but having faith in others, as well as yourself, could save heartache and disappointment

You've probably heard the phrase 'no man is an island'. This pithy aphorism originates in prose by the metaphysical poet John Donne. It continues 'every man is a piece of the continent, a part of the main'. Even though times have moved on since 1624, the date of Donne's work, the sentiment remains the same: you're part of something bigger than yourself. And if that's true, what makes you so connected?

Arguably, one of the most important elements of a friendship is trust. It's also central to romantic relationships, healthcare, the workplace and business transactions. It's even necessary for a sense of self-worth (see overleaf). Would you bank with a company if you thought it was untrustworthy? Would you leave your pet with a friend you knew to be irresponsible? Trust relies on being sure the other person in any transaction or relationship is honest and will do the right thing by you. When it's shaken, it can make human relations difficult, or even risky. But what exactly is this elusive concept?

Trust versus reliance

Some believe trust and reliance are one and the same. After all, they share many features. You might rely on the goodwill of a stranger, and hope they return a lost purse or set of keys. You might trust a friend to give constructive advice about a relationship problem. Both trust and reliance are integral to helping relationships to flourish and form the backbone of many social interactions. What would be the point of going to school if you couldn't believe what the teachers told you? What sense would it make to visit your GP if you couldn't rely on their advice, given research shows that we trust healthcare professionals above other workers?

The two concepts are different, however. Throughout time, societies and cultures worldwide have had different words for trust that have had varying meanings, whereas reliance tends to have one word to express one specific thing. The two also provoke different responses. Feelings of misplaced reliance often relate to less intense emotions, which tend to be self-directed ('I was wrong to rely on you', for example). Misplaced trust, on the other hand, frequently relates to more extreme emotions, such as betrayal ('I trusted you, and you hurt me'). In an article entitled *Trust and Anti-Trust*, philosopher Annette Baier wrote that 'trusting can be betrayed, or at least let down, and not just disappointed'.

Imagine this scenario: you have confidence in a friend, so you decide to ask them to look after your dog while you go to the shops. This belief in them might come from having witnessed their compassion towards a grief-stricken pal and seen their organisational ability in juggling work deadlines with family commitments. The two factors might make them appear the perfect candidate for dog-sitting. In her book *How Can I Be Trusted? A Virtue Theory of Trustworthiness*, philosopher Nancy Nyquist Potter agrees with this thinking. She defines a trustworthy person as someone 'who can be counted on, as a matter of the sort of person he or she is'.

Conversely, you might rely on someone to act badly. You've probably seen compulsive liars on TV and film, like Creed Bratton in the US version of *The Office*. His colleagues could pretty much depend on him to invent a fabrication, but would they trust him to lie? Many philosophers say that trust is a kind of reliance but not mere reliance – because it involves an extra factor. They say this is something like goodwill or benevolence – in other words, you trust someone to act well.

Commitment and risk

Sometimes it's useful to think about things from another angle. Inspiring philosopher Katherine Hawley believed trust was akin to commitment in a relationship. So, when you have faith in someone, you ask them to pledge themselves to do something for you, such as helping with the weekly shopping.

She pointed out that such commitment involved risk, which was part and parcel as to why the process could seem unnerving. Anyone who's ever loaned a friend a much-loved item and been baffled when it wasn't returned will recognise the concern. And it's not just property that can be lost. In some cases, the friendship itself slowly starts to fade. The good news is you can determine the process. One way to think about trust is as a two-way system – you can exert control over what you entrust and to whom. You might want to think about trusting wisely. What does that look like? You could, for example, weigh up previous evidence of trustworthiness before lending someone a sentimental or expensive-to-replace item. What that evidence looks like will depend on the relationship. One place to start might be to explore a friend's transparency. If you've asked them to dog-sit, for example, would they be likely to give you notice if their plans changed and they were no longer able to help? Or would they stay schtum and let you down at the last minute?

Of course, everyone has different strengths. One person might be a great listener, another an intuitive problem-solver and a third a true negotiator. Compiling lists of the most trustworthy friends, however, isn't necessarily the answer. You could instead ask yourself who's the most appropriate or well-qualified friend for a particular job. You wouldn't, for example, depend on a car mechanic to repair your shoes, or a cobbler to fix an engine. Similarly, you'd be more likely to ask a feline-loving friend to cat-sit than you would someone who had a serious aversion to all creatures with claws.

New friendships

All these decisions, of course, are easier to make when you have evidence of previous behaviour to fall back on. But how do you begin to have faith in a new friend? That can be challenging, as clinical psychologist Tamara Scully explains:

'Trust is fundamental to strong positive relationships but it's not something that is there immediately.' In this case, it can help to start small and work your way up. You could lend a new acquaintance a well-read book or much-watched DVD that you don't mind losing, especially if it fits their interests. This will give you an idea as to whether it will be returned. It's important, however, to keep it natural and not force the issue. If, for example, they're going through trying times but choose to be around close family rather than new friends, don't take it personally. As Tamara says: 'Trust is something you build together in small moments of interaction – keeping promises, supporting one another, showing up, apologising if you get something wrong.'

Once you begin to count on one another, you could impart something that holds more personal value, such as a favourite recipe book. For some there might be a temptation to buy expensive new items with the intention of lending them, but try to remember that trust can't be bought. In the words of His Holiness the Dalai Lama, the spiritual leader of Tibet: 'We need friends, and friendship is based on trust. To earn trust, money and power aren't enough; you have to show some concern for others. You can't buy trust in the supermarket.' Sometimes things fall apart, and you might put your faith in someone who lets you down. Trusting again might feel frightening, but ultimately, it's the bridge that connects islands.

Words: **Lizzie Bestow**

If you find that issues of trust are affecting your ability to make friends and maintain relationships, and you'd like to change the situation, it might help to talk to your GP or a counsellor. There are also many online groups and charities that can help, including mind.org.uk.

TRUSTING YOURSELF

Are you a trustworthy person? If you believe the answer is no, you might be failing to perceive yourself as others see you. Here are some pointers to bear in mind

Take time out. Asserting yourself is a step on the path to trusting yourself. Everyone needs time to rest. You don't have to be constantly on call for other people. Of course, if you're in a care-giving role, it might be difficult to get time to yourself, but everyone would benefit from stopping at some point in the day, even if only for five minutes.

Be honest. Try to be candid if friends or family have asked you to take on too much. Of course, it's important to stay polite. If you're struggling to find the words, you could say something like: 'I've got a lot on my plate at work at the moment. Is it okay if you get someone else to dog-sit?' Recognising your needs also means you'll be more attentive to the needs of others.

Follow your goals. Whatever the size or the nature of any intentions you've set for yourself, follow them up. So, if you've decided to read more, put your feet up and go for it; if you want to learn the piano, set aside time to practise; if you're trying to master a new language, get talking. Schedule the time in your diary.

Forgive yourself. It's okay to make mistakes. If a friend trusted you with her expensive camera and you've lost or broken it, don't beat yourself up about it. Instead, be transparent and as upfront about it as soon as possible. Tamara suggests taking time out to explain and apologise.

Believe in yourself. It might be tempting to see rough patches as proof that you can't be trusted. This isn't true. Every time you return after a setback is more evidence that you can weather a storm. Whatever that looks like for you, be it a challenging presentation at work or bravely facing a situation that causes personal anxiety, it reflects your character as a person upon whom others can rely and trust.

ILLUSTRATIONS: TIFFANY DANG

CREATIVITY

'*Books are meat and medicine and flame and flight and flower,*
steel, stitch, and cloud and clout, and drumbeats on the air'

Gwendolyn Brooks

Show time

For many, the experience of watching a musical live on stage is joyful and empowering, even though its story might have sombre undertones. So, what's behind it?

Musical theatre, admittedly, isn't everyone's cup of tea. While enthusiasts will go to see several productions each year, a tag-along friend or family member might be sighing with exasperation before the first scene is out. As hundreds of prisoners grunt in unison (*Les Misérables*) or a workhouse of half-starved orphans find the energy and optimism to sing about the banquet of their dreams (*Oliver!*), you're either fully invested in this melodramatic alternate universe, where everyone bursts into song and dance at the drop of a hat, or you just don't buy it.

Indeed the genre is defined by its fusion of song, dialogue and movement and gives equal importance to each aspect. Western musical theatre is thought to have roots in ancient Greek tragedies and comedies, where music and dance both played a part in open-air performances. And though there's some dispute over the earliest musical, many believe that the first on New York's Broadway was *The Black Crook*, originally performed in 1866. Its creation seems to have been something of a happy accident, occurring when a booked venue suddenly burned down and caused a dance show and dramatic play to be combined at the last minute. While in opera the dancing was left to the troupe, and in burlesque there was usually no storyline, here all three elements of singing, dancing and storytelling were in the mix for the first time, and a new breed of live entertainment was born.

Secret to success

Almost 150 years later, stage musicals have proved themselves to be a cultural mainstay. *The Lion King* is a case in point. It premiered on Broadway in 1997 and has since entranced more than 100 million people around the world, having played at over 100 cities in 20 countries, including at London's West End for more than 20 years. Other even longer running West End shows include *Les Misérables*, from 1985, based on Victor Hugo's novel of the same name, and Andrew Lloyd Webber's *The Phantom of the Opera*, from 1986, which continue to prove their enduring ability to enchant and entertain.

The unabated triumph of musicals such as these can be boiled down to their feel-good factor – the pure, unadulterated joy experienced by their international, inter-generational audiences. West End star Hiba Elchikhe, who plays the protagonist's best friend Pritti Pasha in *Everybody's Talking About Jamie*, can relate to this. She was, in her words, 'obsessed' with shows like *The Lion King* and *Wicked* from a young age, because they never failed to cheer her up. '*Wicked* was my escape from the real world for the longest time. I literally learned every single part on that cast recording. As well as the incredible music, I connected to [protagonist] Elphaba being different and the idea that these differences made her special.'

Seemingly, musicals are able temporarily to relieve anxious minds and transport spectators into other worlds, where witches go to universities at which goats are professors, for example. Yet fantasy aside, musicals are other-worldly by default because of the way speech flows unrealistically into song and vice versa. This requires a willing audience, who can suspend their disbelief and allow themselves to be carried into a different realm. In this dream-like land, connecting with a character, or even just a lyric, makes it feel as if anything is possible.

Making of a musical

Combining the empowering effects of song with an engrossing plot – including believable characters and more than one narrative strand – is the next step. Laurence Connor, director of Andrew Lloyd Webber's West End musical *Cinderella*, as well as UK and US tours of his *The Phantom of the Opera* among other productions, explains how this works in practice: 'The general rule with musicals is that if the emotion or drama hits a point where talking is no longer enough, you sing. I can ramp up emotional tension through song in a way that isn't possible with speech or spoken word. There's more control.'

And, as opposed to dramatic plays, musical narratives are less linear and more layered in structure. They'll often repeat lyrics at different stages of a character's narrative arc to underscore particular themes. 'By playing an early melody in a slightly different way later on in the story, musicals signpost pivotal moments in a character's development without actually saying anything explicitly,'

says Laurence. For example, in Lin-Manuel Miranda's *Hamilton* (see right) the refrains of 'rise up', 'raise a glass to freedom' and 'I am not throwing away my shot' – all used early on in the musical – echo throughout, with their most poignant spectres haunting the penultimate piece, *The World Was Wide Enough*, serving as a reminder of the protagonist's inspiring journey and the hardships he overcame along the way.

Alongside story and song, dance is the third indispensable ingredient that contributes to the overall thrill. Hiba describes how choreography adds real-world detail to the fictional stage-scape of *Everybody's Talking About Jamie*, which tells the coming-of-age story of the eponymous character as he overcomes bullying to become a drag queen: 'The moves the schoolchildren do in the song *Work of Art,* for example, reference voguing, which is massive in the drag community.' These visual symbols and exuberant routines also create a dynamic feast for the eyes, more wholly engaging the senses and enthralling viewers.

There are other subtle ways, such as the use of sound effects and lighting, in which musicals can scale up theatrics to heighten emotion. As a director, Laurence experiments with many technical elements so as to make the score as impactful as possible, deciding whether a song requires the entire company in an all-guns-blazing number or a stripped back, single spotlight set up. The composition and lyrics dictate the rest of the production, which is always artful but not noticeably so. 'Any shifts in tone should be imperceptible,' emphasises Laurence. 'You know those goosebump-inducing moments when you can't quite put your finger on what has changed? If you could, I wouldn't be doing my job right.'

Capturing the human spirit

With their complex, multidisciplinary arrangements, musicals can tell life-affirming stories arguably more intensely than any other stage or screen entertainment, leaving their audiences full of zest for life. Yet many retain an ultimately sombre concern

at their core (see right for more). *Come From Away*, for example, is based on a real-life story that unfolded in the aftermath of the 9/11 attacks in a small Newfoundland town, which took in the passengers of 38 flights when they were diverted from US airspace. The story is inextricable from the shocking and painful events that preceded it, yet the show became the longest-running Canadian musical in Broadway history and transferred to London's West End in 2019. 'When you find the right angle – one that highlights the good of humankind – telling a story like this can still hit home in a positive way,' explains Laurence. Perhaps dire circumstances such as these amplify the innate and precious nature of the human virtues enacted. The story's beacon of hope burns with even greater strength as a result.

While an audience's imaginative escape into a musical's worldview is largely accomplished on stage (and in the orchestral pit), the physical trappings of a live theatre experience should not be forgotten. As Laurence describes: 'As soon as you walk into the plush auditorium, the hustle and bustle of the theatre makes you feel like you are a part of something special and exciting. As the lights dim and the first chords play, you become totally consumed by it.' No phones, no distractions of any kind. 'The magic of musical theatre,' Laurence concludes, 'is that it brings us together in mutual respect and admiration for the level of collaboration and craft showcased by such a production.'

The sheer amount of talent on display is always extraordinary and is sure to further inspire and invigorate an audience – and maybe even win over one or two detractors after all.

Words: Jenny Rowe

Restrictions permitting, Cinderella *will run at the Gillian Lynne Theatre until 13 February 2022.* Everybody's Talking About Jamie *is due to return to London's Apollo Theatre in 2022.*

ILLUSTRATIONS: LIDA ZIRUFFO

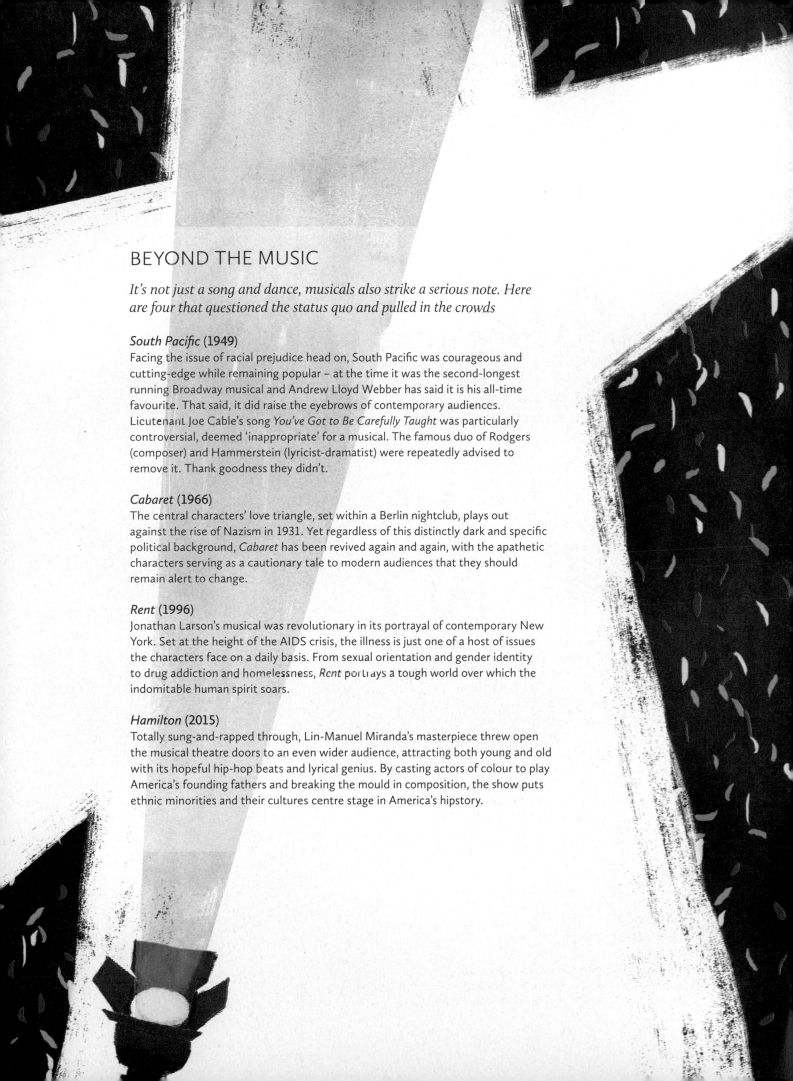

BEYOND THE MUSIC

It's not just a song and dance, musicals also strike a serious note. Here are four that questioned the status quo and pulled in the crowds

South Pacific (1949)
Facing the issue of racial prejudice head on, South Pacific was courageous and cutting-edge while remaining popular – at the time it was the second-longest running Broadway musical and Andrew Lloyd Webber has said it is his all-time favourite. That said, it did raise the eyebrows of contemporary audiences. Lieutenant Joe Cable's song *You've Got to Be Carefully Taught* was particularly controversial, deemed 'inappropriate' for a musical. The famous duo of Rodgers (composer) and Hammerstein (lyricist-dramatist) were repeatedly advised to remove it. Thank goodness they didn't.

Cabaret (1966)
The central characters' love triangle, set within a Berlin nightclub, plays out against the rise of Nazism in 1931. Yet regardless of this distinctly dark and specific political background, *Cabaret* has been revived again and again, with the apathetic characters serving as a cautionary tale to modern audiences that they should remain alert to change.

Rent (1996)
Jonathan Larson's musical was revolutionary in its portrayal of contemporary New York. Set at the height of the AIDS crisis, the illness is just one of a host of issues the characters face on a daily basis. From sexual orientation and gender identity to drug addiction and homelessness, *Rent* portrays a tough world over which the indomitable human spirit soars.

Hamilton (2015)
Totally sung-and-rapped through, Lin-Manuel Miranda's masterpiece threw open the musical theatre doors to an even wider audience, attracting both young and old with its hopeful hip-hop beats and lyrical genius. By casting actors of colour to play America's founding fathers and breaking the mould in composition, the show puts ethnic minorities and their cultures centre stage in America's hipstory.

Could you be a book blogger?

No longer the preserve of paid critics, becoming a book reviewer has never been so accessible – and who knows, your passion might even turn into something more lucrative...

Not so many years ago, the role of book reviewer was a rarefied space that belonged mostly to the inside pages of the press. There was a clear divide between the opinions of the professional and those of the unpaid, yet avid, reader. A decade and a half ago, enthusing about a novel you loved had to be done informally, among friends, and your analysis of plot or characterisation was reserved for a small circle of listeners. Yet a revolution is under way in the world of reviews, propelled, like much of modern life, by the internet.

Creative outlet

If you're the sort of person who can munch through a novel in days, who yearns to share that love with others and who adores delving into the reasons why a particular read works – or doesn't – for you, then becoming a book blogger might be the perfect outlet for your passion. In addition, there's the chance of getting free advance copies months before they're published, as well as the knowledge that your opinion is as sought after as that of the paid critic.

For although positive words from the press are still much cherished, these days they're often used alongside quotes from reputable review sites, run by passionate readers like you. Yet that primary motivation is, as always, to share your love of books – and, by doing so, to forge connections with writers and readers, maintaining a community of like-minded people. In addition, if you've a desire to work in publishing, then running a review site might be a useful route in.

And if you're a budding author yourself, then – as you'll discover overleaf – becoming part of the industry might well give you the confidence to follow your path and live your dream. So if you're a bookworm with a desire to share your passion, how do you alchemise your hobby and become an essential cog within the world of words?

Here four award-winning bloggers share their expertise...

How to get started

You can begin by simply writing reviews of what you've read on your own, easy-to-create, website. Setting up a site is free, relatively straightforward and it can be tailored to your own tastes. Jo Barton started Jaffa Reads Too in 2011 – inspired by her ginger cat Jaffa – and reviewed copies she'd bought for herself. 'It seemed like a fun thing to do,' she says, even though she had 'no technical knowledge of where to start, or indeed of how to maintain, a website.' Wordpress or Blogger, which Jo signed up to, are free platforms that guide newbies through the process. You can use them to share images, write thoughtful critiques and add other pages that interest you, such as Jo's Sunday Brunch author interviews.

Build your reputation by setting up profiles on sites such as Goodreads, Instagram and Twitter, where you can share links to your reviews. Linda Hill, who runs Linda's Book Bag, didn't start out with a grand plan. '[Building my audience] wasn't something I set out to do,' she says. Instead, she used social media in order to make connections with authors, publishers and fellow bloggers. 'I engaged with these people, retweeting their tweets and sharing their posts, and they did the same for me in return. Gradually people began to follow me, and I remember the incredible excitement when I hit a hundred followers on Twitter.' She now has nearly 16,000.

Anne Cater is another titan of the world. As well as running her site, Random Things Through My Letterbox, she reviews for the national press and is a judge for two prestigious awards. She agrees that creating connections is the way to build success and thinks social media can be used more effectively. 'I don't think that just posting a link to a review is enough,' she says. 'It's good to get involved in bookish conversations and follow other people in the community.'

Jo suggests making your site as professional as you can in order to build success. 'A professionally written and diligently maintained site, with a good eye for detail, helps enormously.'

Linda adds: 'For anyone starting out, I wouldn't be too fixated on the number of followers you have or posts' likes and views you get. Follow others, share for them, be enthusiastic and support people. The rest will follow.' Once your reputation starts to grow, you might be offered advance copies of novels or non-fiction works prior to publication. 'The majority on my site have been sent free of charge by the publisher or author,' says Anne. 'I'd advise anyone to get their name out there first, before asking for advance copies. Follow publishers on Twitter – quite often they will Tweet out with offers.' Linda says: 'Remember, you don't have to review brand-new books. Some of my most popular posts have been for older ones.'

Launchpad to a new career

Although running a site is voluntary, your hobby might end up leading to a career in the industry, and perhaps – if you're a budding author – to a publication deal. Noelle Holten is now a bestselling author and publishing PR, but she was a senior probation officer in 2015 when she started CrimeBookJunkie to, as she says, 'connect with people who shared the same interests as me'. After winning various awards for her site and posting regularly – 'I was reliable, and this is key' – she became known to publishers and was offered paid work. 'I think this is what helped me gain a job in the industry,' she says. 'It definitely wasn't my background in probation.' Noelle didn't stop there.

'My experience as a blogger also gave me more confidence to network at festivals and I met a few people who encouraged me to write a book. So I did.' That novel, *Dead Inside*, was the first in a crime series featuring DC Maggie Jamieson. It led to a five-book deal with Harper Collins, became an international Kindle bestseller and garnered praise from authors such as Ian Rankin and Angela Marsons. 'I truly am living the dream,' she says.

Words: **Stephanie Lam**

TIPS FOR A BESTSELLING BOOK BLOG

Be spoiler-free
Linda says: 'In your reviews never retell the story! I tend to comment on the plot in terms of pace. Even saying something like: "You'll never guess the twist at the end" is a spoiler for me.'

Be kind
'Human nature is as it is and I can't enjoy everything,' says Jo. 'Right at the start I decided that I wouldn't post bad reviews so if I don't enjoy something I contact the author and/or publisher directly to let them know that the story didn't work for me.'

Be professional
Noelle says: 'If you commit to [writing] a review, stick to it. I have a diary and make note of the things I have promised. Others use their phone calendars or spreadsheets – whatever is easiest to keep you organised.'

Be yourself
Anne advises: 'Don't try to be like anyone else. Be yourself.' What's paramount, though, is that it feeds you. Linda says: 'Enjoy it. Blogging should be fun.'

For Jo, Linda, Anne and Noelle's blogs, visit jaffareadstoo.blogspot.com, lindasbookbag.com, randomthingsthroughmyletterbox.blogspot.com and crimebookjunkie.co.uk.

FIVE DESTINATION BOOK BLOGS

The Book Trail
As well as a review site, The Book Trail is a vicarious travel agency. Select your next read via the drop-down menu based on your desired location and setting, and you can choose which book to take on your real or virtual holiday. You can request books set anywhere from Antarctica to a Greek island, or ask for settings as diverse as a road trip, an embassy or the city's dark underbelly.
thebooktrail.com

What's Hot?
Beautifully styled photographs of books and places, along with reviews and pieces on literary travel make up the content of award-winning blogger Laura's site. She also writes about being biracial, and campaigns against Chinese and East Asian stereotypes on both her site and her popular Instagram feed.
whatshotblog.com

The Black Book Blog
This new-and-upcoming blog intends, in addition to providing a platform for Black authors, to spotlight books by authors from diverse regions of the world and backgrounds. 'My sole aim with this blog,' writes site owner Rachel, 'is to encourage you all to diversify your bookshelf and give a voice to books that promote individuality of thought.'
theblackbookblogg.com (sic)

The Lesbrary
A site containing around a dozen reviewers living in countries ranging from Canada to Japan. The blog focuses its reviews mainly on bi and lesbian books. You can browse by representation – including neurodiversity and people of colour – or by genre.
lesbrary.com

Hardcover Haven
'Badass bibliophile' Lila is a science student and self-described 'massive extrovert'. Her site includes reviews, a book club focused on diverse voices, and shedloads of enthusiasm. She is also multiply disabled and writes advice for other bloggers on avoiding burnout and on not owing anyone a 'disability story'.
hardcoverhaven121.wordpress.com

Imagine that!

Adults are prone to visualising things through a negative lens, but what happens when you tap into the power of your inner child's imagination?

Do you remember being really young and imagining what it would be like to travel somewhere far away and how much fun that would be? Or how amazing it would be to visit an amusement park? Or dreaming about someday driving a car wherever you wanted to go? I used to do this a lot and spent loads of time drifting off into my imagination, which was a fun place to be back then.

This is because when children use their imagination, they tend towards picturing a good future instead of a bad one, while also visualising the positive emotions that might be felt within their fantasy. Then along comes adulthood and gradually imagination starts being employed in the exact opposite way. Adults tend to use it to envision a not-so-great future and imagine themselves feeling the negative emotions brought about from these fictional outcomes. They might start picturing adverse conflicts and wonder how they're going to manage all the subsequent undesirable feelings.

Reality and reclaiming the fun picture

Of course, there are many understandable reasons why this happens. Previous experiences of difficult encounters or situations come into play and the weight of work, financial or familial responsibility often makes it difficult not to at least consider what might happen if events go awry. Given these factors, it's hardly surprising if our imagination, which was once used as a way to thrill and delight, becomes just another thing that brings on a state of anxiety and stress.

But wouldn't it be great to reclaim its use for feeling good, instead of bad? One way to start doing this is to remember how you felt when you were sitting there as a kid, daydreaming and picturing all the exciting things you were going to do. Not sure how? Try the following four-step visualisation techniques and let your imagination run wild with only fun things:

1. Firstly, imagine how you want to feel before you bring up the scenario. When you focus on the desired feeling, you can then fill in the picture of where it will take place and what you will be doing. Want to feel calm and relaxed? Maybe you'll daydream about reclining on a secluded beach in the sunshine. Want to imagine having a lot of fun? Perhaps you'll visualise going bungee jumping and the feeling of weightlessness you'll have after stepping off the platform. Picture the sensations in your body and try to connect with the feeling first.

2. Don't get too hung up on specifics. Stay with the feeling. Picture general things to begin with, rather than details that might make you get sidetracked with imagined problems.

3. Want to imagine yourself having fun in Paris? Play some French music and start daydreaming. Write in a journal about beautiful things you enjoy. Take photos of flora and fauna you find inspiring. Watch shows about activities you've always wanted to try. Start tuning in more frequently to relaxing, fun images you find appealing. You probably did this as a kid more often than you remember. How often did you stare at books and posters that jump-started your imagination back then? For instance, I had a poster of some ballet pumps on my wall, and every night I'd stare at it and daydream about how fun it would be to be a ballerina. What things captured your attention?

4. Talk to yourself in an encouraging way. It's easy to normalise telling yourself negative things about the future, but as a kid, you're more likely to think along the lines of: 'That's going to be so much fun when I get to do that!' Try to tap into similar language on a daily basis and notice how it makes you feel.

Visualisation is an effective tool that can affect your emotional state. Bring out your inner child by using its power in a more creative way and see where the imaginary adventure leads you.

Words: **Risa Williams**
Risa is a licensed psychotherapist. Her latest book, *The Ultimate Anxiety Toolkit: 25 Tools to Worry Less, Relax More and Boost Your Self-esteem*, is out now. To find out more, visit risawilliams.com.

ILLUSTRATION: HELENA CARTLEDGE

Floral fancies

Dallas-based Alli Koch is a custom artist and designer who's turned her hobby of doodling blooms into a successful full-time business. Here, the Texan tells Breathe *what makes her tick and shares her simple tips for drawing modern florals*

Tell us a bit about you...
Hi, I'm Alli K, full-time artist and owner of Alli K Design. When I graduated, I thought I was destined for a 9-5 job. Little did I know my patience and determination to find a position would turn my art hobby into my dream career. Small paper signs turned into giant painted murals, flower doodles turned into books, and hanging with friends turned into a podcast. Alli K Design has helped me find my purpose, which is to create beautiful art and encourage others to do the same. Teaching and inspiring people keeps me going. Well, that and sweet tea.

As a self-confessed 'plant lady', you're obviously very into flowers and other greenery, what is it about them that resonates with you so much?
I'm a perfectionist at heart, and sometimes it can crimp me when I am creating. But when I think about nature, I don't think about perfection because petals are whimsical and no two flowers are the same. Reminding myself of this helps relieve any pressure I feel to make my illustrations perfect.

How did you get into drawing flowers for a living?
When I started Alli K Design, I was creating custom canvases and wedding invitations and doing loads of calligraphy. To mix up all of the letters, I started drawing flowers. Soon after, my publisher found me on Instagram, and asked if I'd be interested in a how-to-draw flower book. It's been flowers ever since.

We hate to make you pick, but what's your favourite flower?
The anemone because it comes in black and white. But if I could choose two favourites, I would also say the protea, because it has such amazing structure and I love its powerful symbolism.

Take us through your perfect day.
It includes waffle fries, a large sweet tea, warm-enough weather to take the top off my Jeep and a game night with friends.

Who or what inspires you the most?

I gain a lot of energy and motivation from the people around me. My parents (especially my dad) and my creative colleagues are my biggest influences. When I see them achieving their goals, it motivates me to go after and accomplish mine.

What's your favourite project that you've ever done?

Definitely my books, because through them, I can teach people of all ages around the world. They've given people confidence to draw and even start their own business, as well as being an outlet for creative mindfulness. It's crazy for me to think about the impact my books have had and how they're changing the lives of others. It's an honour and an inspiration for me.

What advice do you have for readers who want to turn their hobby or side-hustle into a full-time career?

Think long and hard about what you want. Not to sound like a downer, but the minute you turn your hobby into a job, it's hard to go back to making it something you do just for fun. I hardly just paint for no reason. My mind tends automatically to go into work mode. Since making art my career, I have found other hobbies like pickleball or collage/mix media to rest my mind.

Interview by **Samhita Foria**

Interested to find out more? Turn the page as Alli breaks down the anatomy of a flower and offers tips on drawing blooms from scratch

BEGIN TO BLOOM

Pencils at the ready? Alli takes us through the anatomy of a flower
before outlining three easy-to-follow drawing exercises

First, it's important that we break down the basic elements of what is being drawn before actually putting pen or pencil to paper. Knowing the basic anatomy of a flower will help you to understand the illustrations you will be designing.

A flower has four basic parts: the pistil, the stamen, the petals and the sepals. The pistil is found at the very centre and is often a small, circular shape with an extension from its centre, called the stigma. This is an important part of drawing a flower because it's usually the first thing drawn.

Another part found towards the centre is the stamen, which might look different for each bloom. The centre of a flower is crucial in terms of identifying that flower, similar to the way a thumb print can reveal the identity of a human.

The most recognisable bit to the human eye is the petals. These are the colourful parts that come in a number of shapes and sizes. Finally, the sepals are like leaves that appear at the base of the flower and attach to the stem. You might not see any sepals in the beginning stages of drawing until we start illustrating bouquets.

1. Half part of a flower (the pistil is at the very centre)
2. Petal
3. Stamen and sepals
4. Stamen

Learning curves

Now that you know exactly what you will be drawing, it's time to look at how you will be drawing it. Keep in mind that anyone (yes, anyone!) can do this. Real or certified art skills are not required. What you do need is the ability to draw line letters, specifically an 'S' and a 'C'.

The main shapes you'll be making for these modern florals are called 'S-curves' and 'C-curves'. These are exactly what they sound and look like – the curves in the letters 'S' and 'C'. Each floral illustration is really just a number of both put together.

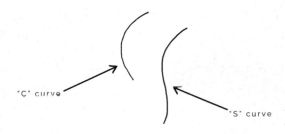

These curves are used to create the basic outline of the flower and to give shape and definition to the flat image you have just created. With curved lines, you can create shadows on certain parts of your bloom that will bring it to life. In the art world, it's called line shading. The closer the lines are together, the darker the shadow; the more spread out the lines, the lighter the shadow.

The trick to remember here is that to effectively give shape to your flower, your shading must follow the same direction as the lines and curves of the part you're focusing on. You can't create definition using straight lines, and you can't create good definition using lines that are curved in the opposite direction of the part of the flower they are beside. To make your petals look curved, the curves of your shading have to go with the outer curve of the petal.

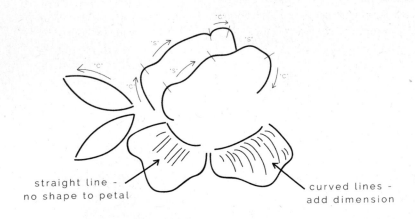

Ready to give it a go? Turn over to learn how to draw three classic florals in a pared-back, contemporary style

DAHLIA

The flower of forever

1 We are going to be drawing a side angle of the dahlia, so we'll start it a bit different from the others. Because the main centre of the flower will not be visible from this side angle, we are going to start by drawing the three small leaves coming off the base of the flower. These leaves are pointing downward and have a rounded point at the end. The petals of a dahlia create a large cup shape. Draw two or three petals coming out from either side of the base of the flower in a wing-like motion.

2 Begin to fill in the flower with more petals, making them smaller and shorter the closer they get to the centre. These petals are all overlapping, so you will not be able to see all of each petal.

3 To finish the main shape of the flower, continue to draw more petals behind the ones you have already drawn by making them appear smaller as they get further away from the edge of the flower closest to you. You can also start to add in a few folds to the petals at the base of the flower to show the cradle or cup shape.

4 To add shape and definition to the dahlia, draw three to five lines along the curves of each of the petals. Alternate between long and short, remembering to allow the line to curve in the same direction that the petal would be curving. For the petals that are folding, your shading lines inside will be closer together and point in one direction, while the shading lines on the outside of the petal will be further apart and curving in a different direction.

HYDRANGEA

The flower of gratitude

1 To start drawing a hydrangea, create a half-dome on your page in pencil. You will want to be able to erase this once it's been filled with petals.

2 Next, add a small stem to the straight edge of your dome with a smaller off-shooting stem. You are now going to fill the dome with a multitude of smaller flowers. Each will have a tiny circle in the centre with four oval-shaped petals. The edges of these are smooth and round. Draw several large versions of these flowers in your dome.

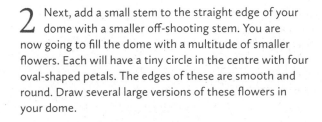

3 Continue to fill in the dome until it looks full. Create the effect of the flowers overlapping each other by drawing some smaller flowers and some incomplete flowers in the extra blank space in and around your dome.

4 For shading, add several small tick marks coming from the middle of each petal with a few longer curves that follow the curve of the petal. Erase any of the dome that's still visible from Step One, and you are done.

Turn over for another flower variety, as well as some space to practise drawing your blooms

CAMELLIA

The flower of perfection

1 The centre of a camellia starts with three small buds, which are similar to the shape of a balloon – rounder on one end and coming together to a point at the other end.

2 In the next few steps, you'll be filling in the rest of the flower with C-curves or loops to create petals that all build off each other. It is usually easiest to start with an anchor petal near the top and then work your way around clockwise.

3 Make another layer of petals, starting with one main anchor petal near the top and working your way around the flower. Some will appear to be behind others to add to the layered look. The edges of these petals are more rounded and smoother than the petals of a peony or a ranunculus, but they are still not perfectly rounded.

4 Continue to go around the circle of petals, adding C-curves to each layer. Each layer should be organic because there isn't a certain number of petals. The layers towards the centre will be closer together, and each layer of petals will get slightly bigger as they get further away from the centre.

5 Feel free to continue to add layers until your flower is the size you want it to be. Once you feel like your camellia is finished, your final layer will close off the gaps between petals with smaller petals to create the illusion that those outermost petals are tucked behind all the others.

6 Because of all the layers of the camellia, the shading of the petals is important to really show the bends and curves of the flower. Each petal will need a series of small lines and curves that start from the centre of the flower. Remember to curve the lines in whatever direction you want your petals to go. Also, remember to draw the lines closer together wherever you want to create more shadow, particularly where the petals are overlapping.

PHOTOGRAPHS: MORGAN CHIDSEY, A SEA OF LOVE. FLORALS PROVIDED BY BOWS AND ARROWS FLOWERS

DOODLE PAGE

Use this space to try out some of your new-found drawing skills

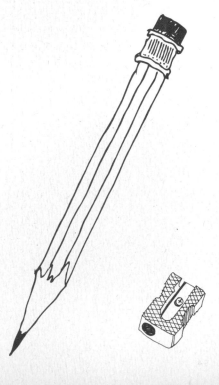

Edited extract from How to Draw Modern Florals *by Alli Koch, published by Blue Star Press, RRP £16.99. Available online and in book shops.*

Listen, hear

People and places convey much more than words, and paying attention to everything they're saying can boost creativity as well as personal development

Listen is a word with many associations. What does it bring to mind for you? An appeal to tune in to a beautiful song? A command to be quiet and pay attention? A punctuation point at the start of a joke? The skill of listening and hearing what others say, or taking in sounds from around us as well as from within us, can be an undervalued process – although not by M Scott Peck, author of *The Road Less Travelled*, who wisely observes: 'You cannot truly listen to anyone and do anything else at the same time.'

The action itself is a broad church with diverse purposes – such as listening to understand, to be informed, for enjoyment and to learn. How we tune in and what we comprehend from the vibration of sound can vary widely too, and studies suggest most people remember between only 25 and 50 per cent of what they hear. So, it seems this is something that we can all benefit from improving – one vital way to be better at it is to practise active listening. That can mean making a conscious effort to hear the words that someone is saying as well as the complete message they're conveying. Becoming a better listener can also benefit work relationships and help to avoid conflict and misunderstandings. It can also connect you to and develop your creativity.

Sound of silence
A leading advocate of using listening as a creative tool is Julia Cameron, author and teacher behind book and creative recovery programme *The Artist's Way*. Julia has helped many to kickstart or renew their practice – and her latest book has the self-explanatory title *The Listening Path: The Creative Art of Attention*. It is, she says, 'deeper' than *The Artist's Way*. This guide is devoted to honing listening in six areas, such as your environment, people around you, and to silence – a profound aspect of the skill. As Japanese writer Haruki Murakami says: 'Silence, I discover, is something you can actually hear.'

Julia began to focus on listening and its connection to creativity after moving from Manhattan – and its 'never-ending sound of honking, sirens and noise' – to a small mountain village in Santa Fe, New Mexico, 'where it's so quiet I can hear a truck rumbling on the road a mile away'. She began to appreciate the benefits of learning to listen fully: 'When we do that, our attention is heightened and we gain healing, insight, clarity. Above all, [listening] creates connections and ignites creativity.' The skill, she realised, had been central to her own output of 40 artistic works, including novels, books, plays and musicals. 'When people would ask me how I was so prolific, I'd say: "I listen." That's my experience – I listen and "hear" what I should be doing next.'

Alternative view
Listening is often considered to be a passive activity, a gap in the conversation when you're not speaking and take a back seat, but Julia doesn't see it that way. 'Some see listening as passive, yielding and giving – not expressive or giving out. It is both. It's being alert to sounds that are intrusive and open to delightful sounds.' Julia teaches students to be alert to one of the most destructive forces to creativity, the inner critic, that negative, nagging voice that says you're not good enough, you can't do it. She suggests that rather than pushing the negative voice down it can help to acknowledge it. 'When your inner critic says: "You're so boring" or "You're no good", you say: "Thank you for sharing," and keep on writing or, if you're acting, you step right past it on to the stage.'

Part of communication
As an actor and voice-over artist, Emilija Ellen is acutely aware of the role listening plays in creativity, and in her life in general. After drama school, Emilija trained in the work of Sanford Meisner, an acting technique rooted in the skill. 'Meisner focused on living in the moment and taught listening with all your body, not just your ears, because there's [a difference between that] and hearing,' she says. 'I realised many people think they're listening but they're not, myself included. As an

actor I had to learn how to really listen, hear what was being said and let that thought land in my body.'

Emilija also agrees with Julia's views on the subject. 'Julia says actors "always listen for the next thing, creatively" and that's so true. You do the work from the inside out, by listening to yourself. Then you get on stage and put your full attention on the other person and the magic happens.' Emilija says she has 'come to value listening more than speaking, as well as the part that silence plays in communication. Listening might seem silent but it is a vital part of communicating, as it's in that silence that you really listen.'

These skills have been invaluable for Emilija's public speaking and workshops. 'I learned to listen very carefully to the audience, scanning them to respond to their needs and mood. It's active. I realised it's not about me, it's about the group's needs. This has helped me to surrender, calm down, have fun with it and hit that flow.'

Power of silence

Emilija has found that spending more time at home and not being constantly occupied with busy activities has given her a fresh perspective, especially in the sounds around her. 'So much of my everyday life was filled with external noise, I was always listening to podcasts or documentaries online. This past year has been a conscious journey of listening to myself, and that includes to my intuition. Trusting that silence is not silence. When there's no TV, radio or online noise, all of a sudden you hear a bird or a thought or the music you listened to as a teenager or your mother's voice from when you were a child, just as it sounded to you then. That has been beautiful.'

Out of this period of deeper listening, Emilija and her friend Jo Darrall, an artist and comic, have created a podcast called The Creative Wanderer. It's an entertaining and insightful look at creativity, which so far has focused on *The Artist's Way* and its potential for unlocking creativity, something the pair have done successfully. The good news is we can all work on reconnecting to and fully realising our listening skills (see right), which, in turn, can bring us the infinite rewards of silence.

Words: **Beverley D'Silva**

The Listening Path: The Creative Art of Attention – A Six Week Artist's Way Programme *by Julia Cameron is available now.*

ILLUSTRATIONS: CHIARA LANZIERI. PHOTOGRAPH: SHUTTERSTOCK.COM

ESCAPE

'Live in each season as it passes; breathe the air, drink the drink, taste the fruit, and resign yourself to the influence of the earth'

Henry David Thoreau

Green shoots of discovery

Growing a tree is not just wonderful for the environment – it's personally satisfying to watch it flourish from seed to sapling and beyond

Deeply affected by the demise of many of the UK's elm trees in the 1970s, novelist Sheila Jeffries pledged that on each birthday she would plant a tree seed for each year of her life. Over the years that have followed, she has joyfully raised many specimens. Sheila, whose rural Somerset garden is full of pots containing foraged beechnuts, walnuts, acorns and more, says: 'My first experience of growing a tree was when I picked up a shiny conker I found in a city park. I still recall my sense of wonder as I watched it germinate and grow.'

It's this fascination, interwoven with concern for loss of habitat, that motivated Sheila and her husband Ted to plant a 'forest of dreams' on a 50-acre site in Cornwall. Over the course of 10 years, and with just two spades, a wheelbarrow and a collection of saplings grown from gathered seeds, they have nurtured this plantation to create a precious, young forest.

It's a heart-warming and inspiring story, but Sheila is aware that most people are unlikely to be in a position to set up such large-scale projects. That said, she's keen to point out that raising even a single tree can make a difference, and not only for the environment. On a personal level, the experience of seeing that first green shoot emerging is miraculous, speaking of hope and renewal.

Luciana Corp, co-director of UK-based, not-for-profit organisation Fellowship of the Trees, would more than likely agree. The group invites people to become tree guardians and Luciana has seen first-hand the perks that follow. 'Apart from the environmental benefits of healthy tree cover, we understand the close relationship that humans need with nature for mental wellbeing,' she says. 'Growing trees from seeds is a great starting point in deepening this connection. It provides a way to have contact with nature, which is accessible to all, bringing a sense of contribution, stewardship and community.'

Virtue of patience – and letting go

Whether your seeds are a gift or the product of careful and respectful foraging, growing a tree takes time, and the results are uncertain. 'Depending upon the species, some seeds require stratification [layering in a moist medium like sand to preserve or help them to germinate], to mimic nature's cycles, while others can be planted straight away,' says Luciana. 'Even in nature, not all seeds will germinate and this stands true when home-growing as well. Patience is required and time will tell whether they'll sprout.' In many ways, this nurturing is an exercise in letting go of expectation. The outcome is something beyond personal control no matter how much TLC is administered. It's a wonderful example of how people can respond to events in their own lives by not attaching themselves to the outcome. It's also a reminder that seeds can be seen as unrealised potential, and if it's meant to be, they'll grow and mature in their own good time.

There is, however, much that can be done to give them the best possible chance of life. 'Before you begin lovingly planting those golden acorns or pine seeds in pots, you must be prepared to protect them from all the wild creatures who'll eat them, given half a chance,' says Sheila. 'Birds, mice, rabbits and others will enjoy the meal, and, if the seed makes it through the winter and sends up a tender little shoot in the spring, the slugs will be ecstatic.' One slug or snail can eat about 20 baby trees in one

night, 'so either keep them in a cool, mouse-free greenhouse or, if they're outdoors, under a wire cage. You can use vine sleeves over individual pots, but even this tough mesh can be chewed by a determined squirrel or a magpie'.

To see a green sapling reaching for the light is wonderful but it's just the start of a long journey. 'Once the seeds have germinated, they need intensive care through their first two years, especially in dry summers,' says Sheila. 'Weed them, shade them and water them daily, and you'll be rewarded with robust little trees. It's a brilliant gift to Mother Earth.'

Get going
You can obtain free seeds from organisations such as Fellowship of the Trees, but if you'd like to find your own, autumn is a good time to go out foraging in woodlands and parks. There are five types of seed: nuts, pods, wings, cones/bracts and fruit pips/stones. You might be familiar with some, such as acorns, hazelnuts and horse chestnuts (conkers). Others, such as those of rowan, blackthorn or elder, might not be as recognisable. If you're not sure about the varieties, take an identification guide when foraging. Examine the seeds carefully to ensure there's no visible damage or infestation before putting the healthiest ones in a paper bag and labelling it accordingly.

Get prepping
Some seeds, such as horse chestnut, oak, sycamore and goat willow, don't require pre-germination treatment and can be planted into soil straight away. Others, such as beech, black walnut and alder, benefit from or require a stratification period, which imitates nature's conditions to overcome dormancy and promote germination.

There are two stratification methods – warm and cold – and the process varies depending upon the species. For both options, the seeds are first placed in a clearly labelled and dated container of slightly moist horticultural sand. Next, they are either left at room temperature or placed in a fridge for a period of time, which, depending upon species, could be anything from four to 40 weeks. Some seeds, such as small-leaved lime, holly and wild cherry, benefit from going through both methods, usually starting with the warm process.

Get sowing
Check seeds often for signs of germination and sow them as soon as a root appears. Luciana says one option is to upcycle any one-litre milk or juice cartons you have to hand. Make sure they're sterilised before laying them horizontally (you'll need to punch through some drainage holes) and filling with free-draining, organic (peat-free) compost mixed with sand. Alternatively, use 20cm eco-friendly pots.

Plant five small seeds in each container. If it's a nut, it will need its own pot. As a guide, to ensure optimum growing conditions, sow seeds to the same depth as their diameter. For example, birch seeds with a 1-2mm diameter require only a slight covering of soil whereas larger acorns with a 1-2cm diameter are sown about 2cm deep. If possible, place outside in a shady area and protect them from hungry creatures. Check them regularly and keep the soil moist but well-drained.

Get planting
When the seedlings are about 5cm tall, replant into extra-deep rose pots. Slow-growing trees, such as oak, can be left for a couple of years, while faster-growing species, such as birch, might need potting on after a year, either to a temporary spot to grow more freely or to their final home where they can mature.

An ideal time to move trees is late autumn. If you have the task of replanting, take great care not to damage the roots and stems, and make sure the roots don't dry out at any point.

If you're raising trees as part of a tree conservation project, your saplings might already have a good home waiting for them. Otherwise, donate them to local tree planting schemes or you could even look into following Sheila's example and take steps to plant a magical forest of dreams as a legacy for future generations.

Words: Carol Anne Strange

For more information about Sheila's Forest of Dreams, visit sheilajeffries.com, while further details of Luciana's work can be found at fellowshipofthetrees.org. Tree planting projects and tips can also be found at wildseedproject.net, tree-nation.com and treegrowing.tcv.org.uk.

SEEDS OF HAPPINESS

Try your hand at raising these species

Hazel

In mid- to late-September, collect hazelnuts directly from the tree when they're easy to remove from the husk. Put the nuts in water. If they sink, they have a good chance of growing. Discard any that float. Mix a handful of nuts with an equal amount of horticultural sand and place in a container with good drainage. Leave in the shade, away from mice. At the end of February, check for signs of germination. Sow two seeds per pot, about 2cm deep. Water them, keeping the soil moist.

Silver birch

In late August and during September, gather seeds (known as strobiles) from the silver birch tree. Place them in a cotton bag and soak in cold water for up to 48 hours before allowing them to dry. Then pop them in a plastic bag containing moist sand and refrigerate for four weeks to aid germination. In April, sow up to 10 seedlings per pot. Birch grow quickly, so be prepared to repot or plant within the year.

Scots pine

It's not easy to access pine cones directly from the tree so look for cones that are freshly dropped on the ground and still contain their seeds. Although pretreatment isn't required, germination can be improved with four weeks of cold stratification before the intended sowing date. Mix seeds with moist sand and place in a plastic bag in the fridge. In April, sow thinly into trays and cover with a fine layer of sand. Repot in the autumn and, after two years, plant the saplings in the earth.

English oak

In autumn, gather clean, undamaged acorns from the ground. Place them in water. Keep the ones that sink. No pretreatment is required as the seeds germinate naturally and quickly in damp conditions. Plant an acorn about 2cm deep into a small pot of organic (peat-free) compost that has adequate drainage. Alternatively, sow direct into the earth (about 5cm deep).

Legends of the fall

Writers have waxed lyrical about autumn's natural beauty and vibrant hues,
and the science behind the change in leaf colour is just as awe-inspiring

'Every leaf speaks bliss to me, fluttering from the autumn tree'

EMILY BRONTË

A yellow leaf shines brightly in the morning light, although its stem has the strength to adhere to an oak tree's branch for only a few more moments. A rush of wind finally breaks this remnant free from the structure's clutches, swirling it through the air until it lands on top of a pile of crisp leaves at your feet.

It's autumn, a time when forests produce myriad colours that culminate in remarkable displays to delight the senses. Fall is anticipated across the world for this reason, with the season occurring in the Northern Hemisphere from September to November, and in the Southern Hemisphere usually from March to May. Its rainbow display can seem magical, but there are fascinating scientific explanations for the altering scenery.

All change

As autumn arrives, the leaves of deciduous trees begin to look different as they lose their exuberant, green summer growth and take on a dry, crisp-like texture. This alteration is accompanied by dazzling copper-gold tones that radiate across the countryside. The reason for the annual spectacle is survival. Broadleaf species cannot continue to grow and prosper in freezing winter conditions, because their leaf cells would rupture, and photosynthesis – the chemical process that allows plants to produce energy – would be hampered.

These changes are something in which John O'Keefe, scientist and emeritus coordinator of the Fisher Museum at Harvard Forest in the US, has much experience. 'Deciduous trees have evolved to seasonally drop all their leaves and go dormant when sufficient water is not available, because of frozen conditions or a prolonged dry season,' he says. 'Part of this process involves the breakdown of chlorophyll, the green pigment that enables photosynthesis.' The gradual variation in colour of the landscape follows this natural development, as the reduction of emerald shades, created by the presence of chlorophyll, allows the dazzling pigments associated with autumn to become visible. John explains: 'Carotenoids, the yellow pigments

present during the growing season but masked by the green chlorophyll, provide the golden colours seen as the chlorophyll breaks down. Anthocyanins, red pigments produced using energy from sunlight during the fall, create the orange, red and purple colours. The shades seen depend upon the abundance of each present and will change as the process progresses.'

Riot of colour

Carotenoids and anthocyanins are the natural complexion of the plant tissue responsible for autumn colour. Mature displays can be seen in ancient European woodland, as foliage transformation occurs in abundance, with beech, oak and silver birch creating a diverse yellow-copper canopy. In the US and Canada, mixed-species parades of broadleaf and evergreen trees, such as pines, form across the landscape producing a jigsaw of avocado and flame-like colouring. 'In north-eastern US, sugar maples, with their fiery red-orange colour, probably contribute the most to vivid fall displays,' says John. 'Red maples (bright red), birches (yellow), ash (purple), black cherry (pink) and hickories (yellow-gold) provide variety and contrast.' Along with wild species, ornamental specimens are much-admired at this time of year. Standout examples include 25m-tall maidenhair trees native to China, which produce golden hues, tupelo trees from North America with their ovate red-yellow leaves, and the variating ruby foliage of cherry trees.

But while the regularity of autumn can be guaranteed, the same cannot be said for its intensity, which is influenced by growing conditions and weather. The most desirable for colour development are bright days with plenty of sunshine. 'For a healthy tree going into fall, average rainfall and gradually cooling temperatures allow colours to steadily develop, and ample sunlight is especially important for anthocyanins,' says John. 'Cool nights and sunny days are ideal, and a lack of storms and strong winds help to prolong the display.'

Equally as awe-inspiring as this display of colour is a tree's ability to detach and drop its leaves from its branches, a feature

that ensures broadleaf species live to the following year, as John describes: 'Deciduous trees have evolved to respond to decreasing day length and cooling temperatures in autumn to begin the process of dormancy. This includes colour changes in preparation for dropping their leaves, as the chlorophyll is broken down and its compounds are stored in the buds to be used in the new leaves the following spring.'

The process by which leaves separate from the tree is called abscission. 'At the point where the leaf is attached to the stem and the bud for next year's leaf has developed, a layer of barrier cells [the abscission layer] forms,' says John. 'As these cells grow, the connection between leaf and stem decreases until, eventually, the cells form a barrier, the connection is broken and the foliage falls off.'

Earthly powers
But where do these lush layers that carpet the forest floor go? After all, come spring they're often nowhere to be seen. Kirsty Elliott, an environmental scientist and a member of the British Society of Soil Science, explains: '[They're] broken down through a process called decomposition.' This decaying of organic matter can happen in several ways. 'The

first is detritivore fragmentation, where organisms, such as earthworms, ants, flies and millipedes, consume the dead leaves,' she says. 'The second is saprotroph decomposition, where fungi and bacteria produce enzymes to break down leaves into smaller constituents, including simple sugars, water, nutrients and minerals.' In this way, the annual leaf fall boosts the organic matter in the soil system, which is essential to the health of the planet. 'It's vitally important for replenishing nutrients that are depleted when plants grow,' says Kirsty.

'Think of it as nature's recycling process. It's a circular system that sustains levels of important soil nutrients as well as contributing carbon to maintain soil structure and functioning. Without it, soils would become exhausted and unable to sustain life.' So, next time you see autumn leaves on the breeze, take a moment to appreciate their pigments, knowing that while their dazzling display of colour might be over, their work is far from done. They'll be absorbed into the soil, allowing the continuation of life, and another rainbow fall next year.

Words: Alice Johnson

LEAVES LIKE THESE

Five top places to witness nature's wonders

Ontario, Canada

Offering landscapes swathed in vivid colour, the province's popular destinations include the Bruce Peninsula and Spencer Gorge Conservation Area (*right*), situated on the Niagara Escarpment. Algonquin Provincial Park provides another great place to marvel at the autumn landscape with its intense colour display, thanks to its red and sugar maples, bright cherry trees, yellow-leaved birches and coniferous pines. Visit from mid-September through October.

White Mountains, US

Ranging from New Hampshire to Maine, the White Mountains reach across 140km of the US and form a part of the Appalachian range. The maple trees are its autumn stars, as they create a peppering of bright red across the landscape. Visit from late-September until mid-October.

New Forest National Park, UK

Located in Hampshire, this national park features historic woodland, open heathland and pasture. Once used by William the Conqueror as a royal hunting ground, the forest is famous for its deer and ponies, which now roam freely. Ancient deciduous trees, including beech and oak, create a sumptuous display of hues from deep browns to orange, with a shimmering added from silver birches and their yellowing leaves. Visit during October and November.

Tokyo, Japan

To witness the bright-yellow spectacle of maidenhair trees, also known as Ginkgo biloba, visit the 300m-long Ginkgo Avenue in Meiji Jingu Gaien Park, Tokyo. Enjoy the custom of treading on the golden foliage dropped from around 150 of these trees during the annual fall festival, which usually runs from mid-November into December. Ueno Park is another must-visit place to appreciate autumn in the city.

New York, US

This world-famous city offers mixed species that produce a warming autumn glow. The Mall at Central Park (*left*) is lined by American elms that create a sunshiny show of yellow before the cold of winter sets in. Cherries, birches, oaks and the yellow-red variation of the tupelo tree are also found in the park. Visit during October and early November.

Bon voyage!

*Cruise around the world without leaving your
seat through some of our favourites from 2020's
Travel Photographer of the Year competition*

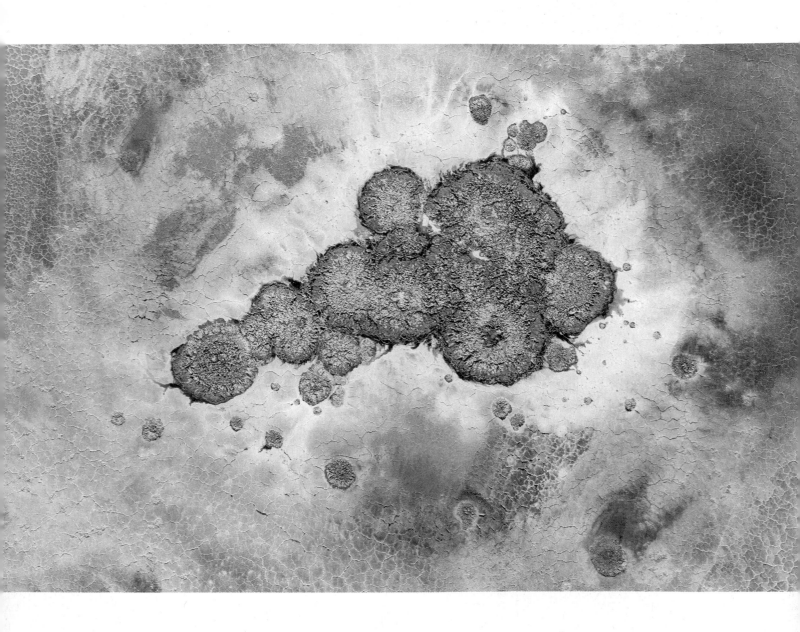

Paul Sansome, UK

Long Bien, Hanoi, Vietnam

(*Opposite*) I had to exercise extreme patience to achieve this shot at a very busy junction in Hanoi, where traffic from left, right and behind me would constantly block the desired image. I waited for an hour before, as I had hoped, just a single bike rode past part of the world's longest mosaic mural, producing an image that I call *Green Energy*.

Scott Portelli, Australia

Kati Thanda-Lake Eyre, South Australia

(*Above*) This is Australia's largest salt-lake, yet it is only covered with water every eight years on average. The vast salt plain dominates the landscape with patterns left behind by the receding water. Natural bore springs emerge across the plains, creating enormous patterns of pastel-blues, yellows and reds as water pushed up through the salt crust creates visual anomalies.

Vladimir Alekseev, Russia

Myanmar

(*Above*) Travel photography doesn't always capture a landscape
or a reportage. Very often it captures a macro world. These
are elements of what surrounds us – the little joys in life to
which we don't pay attention at home.

Wenming Tang, China

Poyang Lake, Jiangxi, China

(*Above*) Located in the north of Jiangxi Province, Poyang Lake
is the largest freshwater lake in China and provides a seasonal
home for more than 100 species of migratory birds, including
11 endangered species.

Jonathan Stokes, UK

Bar Las Teresas, Seville, Spain

(*Above*) Three men sit at a small table in animated conversation,
among a cluttered interior of old posters and paintings,
plates and baskets for food, and a row of jamón hanging
above the bar counter.

Mouneb Taim, Syria

Saraqib, Syria

(*Above*) 27 March 2019: On the occasion of the International
Day of Theater, puppeteer Walid Rashed acts out his show
for children. Since 2013, theatre artist Walid has been touring
devastated neighbourhoods and refugee camps to perform
puppetry and shadow play for Syrian children.

To see more of the winners' gallery, or for information about 2021 Travel Photographer of the Year awards, visit tpoty.com.

Step by (slow) step

Walking to solve any issue might be an ancient concept, but it's as relevant as ever today. And done with a heightened awareness, it can offer a closer connection to nature, too

There's a lovely Latin phrase, solvitur ambulando, which broadly translates as 'it is solved by walking'. It's an idea that's hard to argue with. Stepping outside and placing one foot in front of the other unknots the mind, improves circulation and strengthens a meaningful connection with the outdoors. This is as true in the green heat of springtime as it is in the leaf-litter days of the darker months. But the upsides don't end there. If you walk regularly, certain paths can become as comforting and familiar as old friends. To know a particular route intimately – to understand its quirks and notice its thousands of details – is to be gifted the potential for fresh joy year-round.

This is why, during recent times when there has been a narrowing of geographical horizons, I resolved to become better acquainted with a footpath that passes close to my home. The path is, in many ways, a typical country trail: a quiet, puddly, hedgerow-lined route on the outskirts of an English village. It skirts a farmer's field, passes alongside a small river, then crosses three overgrown meadows to reach a thick patch of woodland. The total distance – there and back – stretches to around 5km.

I resolved to follow this same route daily for seven days, focusing on a specific sense or theme on each walk. The idea was to develop a more mindful attitude towards my own tiny corner of the world map. This is how the week unfolded…

Day one

Sight

When you make a conscious decision to pay attention to what's in front of you, it's extraordinary just how much there is to spot. Branch-filtered sunlight creating fractured shapes on the path. Glossy ivy leaves traced with gossamer veins. Hawthorn berries red as sweets. A perched robin with button-black eyes, still but not quite, its beak twitching and breast quivering. All this was in the first 10 metres.

In eyes-wide mode, it also becomes natural to slow down. The sky was full of long, white cumulus drifting lazily. The surface of the river, when I reached it, was a dancing, drifting, eddying thing, constantly changing. A grey willow on one bank, old and twisted with splayed boughs, waylaid me for ages; every

square inch of its trunk was something to stare at. Up in the woods, meanwhile, I was moving so unhurriedly that – for the first time I could remember – I noticed a pair of up-close roe deer before they noticed me. This initial walk took an almost comical length of time to complete. It was also hugely enjoyable.

Day two

Sound

Today was all about listening. It was the beat of my own feet that I was aware of first. Overnight rain meant my boots sploshed and squelched with each step. But in the same way that the tick-tock of an old-fashioned clock blends into the soundscape, the rhythm of my footsteps soon tuned out. Other sounds started to flood in: loud welters of birdsong, the underlying hum of a distant flour mill, the fluid chuckle of the river. I passed a stand of fir trees and my presence set off a suddenly riotous flapping of wings, which I heard but didn't see.

Listening with intent meant the volume of everything seemed to be amplified. Where the river flowed past a fallen log, the effect seemed as loud as a weir, and when I walked through a five-barred gate, the metal latch swung back into place with a deafening clank. In the woods, where twigs snapped and leaves rustled, the sounds were somehow both clearer and more muffled – and the longer I stood there, the more layers of noise there were to pick out. A quiet day soon morphed into a kind of freeform orchestra.

Day three

Smell

Walking with a focus purely on what could be smelled was, I'll admit, a complete novelty for me. In the fullness of spring or summer, the experience would likely have presented obvious cues at every turn. Not so in an English winter, but that didn't stop the walk being engaging. The scents were cold and earthy, and hard to define. They also held locked-away memories. At one point I had a fully formed flashback to being a muddy-

kneed boy on the school sports field. As is often the way with fleeting smells, the recollection was there one moment and gone the next.

A handful of leaves gave off a dry, peaty aroma. A fir tree had a faint piny tang. Strangely, whenever I stopped and breathed deeply, I had split-second wafts of green and vibrant fields, as though something was blowing in from another season. And in the woods, when I closed my eyes and inhaled there seemed nothing to identify at first, then a kind of mushroomy scent appeared, and beyond that – from somewhere – the sharper smell of woodsmoke, so faint that it felt like a secret discovery.

Day four

Touch

This was another walk that surprised me. It placed my attention onto things that I would usually overlook: the swoosh of the high grass on my legs, the feel of the runkled texture of an oak trunk, the almost imperceptible patter of light rain on my coat, the way that every step of a country lane feels different underfoot. Most of all, I was aware that the breeze on my face was always changing, second by second. It was sometimes soft, sometimes strong, but never constant.

At a wooden footpath signpost, I stopped and ran my fingers over a sheen of green moss. It felt as smooth as the baize of a pool table. Naturally, because the focus was on touch, throughout the walk I found myself concentrating almost entirely on what was close at hand. With the exception of the wind and rain, everything I noticed and dwelt on was within arm's reach, which again brought a new dimension to a familiar path.

Day five

Break of dawn

It was a shade or two above pitch-black when I set out along the path. The morning was chilly, but sporadic birdsong still tumbled from the branches. I'd chosen to do a break-of-dawn walk because I wanted to experience the route at a time I never normally did, when day was just beginning its cycle. And of all the seven walks, this was the most rewarding, purely in terms of the richness of the moment.

There was a wonderful crisp stillness in the air, with low mist on the fields. Early on, a three-carriage train trundled by in the far distance, lights ablaze like the Polar Express. A lone star twinkled in a sky that over the course of an hour moved gradually from purple to the softest of yellows, and in the half-light the woods looked like rainforest. When I reached

the trees, it was an utter joy to stand and watch life stir around me: hares, woodpeckers and squirrels. This, again, was a walk that lasted a long time.

Day six

Nightfall

Whereas the previous day's walk was about watching the world wake up, this was the opposite – witnessing the shutters of night come down. A glimmer of daylight remained when I set off, although by the time I'd walked for 20 minutes, the countryside was just a set of dim half shapes. The evening was cloudy, moonless and calm, but it was hard to fight a slight feeling of jumpiness. Every rustle in the hedgerows gave me a jolt. My senses, without any conscious effort on my part, had moved to full alert.

Perhaps surprisingly, it was only when I got to the woods and stood still that any sense of nerviness dissipated. Being able to stop, and to breathe, made me feel more rational. Taking deep lungfuls of dark forest, and being present, helped me see the experience as something new and fascinating rather than menacing. This feeling lasted while I walked home, stepping through soggy mud, my night-vision now more attuned to the landscape.

Day seven

What does this path mean to me now?

Following this trail for the seventh day in a row, I tried to weigh up whether the path now felt different. The first thing to strike me, a little ridiculously perhaps, was a sense of ownership – as though these were now my trees, my birds, my fields. But when I thought about this more clearly it was really just another way of expressing that I felt better connected to this stretch of land. It seemed easier to tune in to the sounds and sights along the way.

I also realised early on that rather than being some sort of reprise or finale, this seventh walk was simply another chance for a fresh experience. None of the previous six walks had produced the same late-afternoon light, or the same crunch of frost underfoot. In the woods I noticed clusters of sloes for the first time, and the tiny buds on the bare branches of the trees. And the climax? When I was just two minutes from home, the pale shape of a barn owl appeared, quartering the hedgerow in the distance. I've lived in the same house for a decade but, hand on heart, this was a first. Maybe my eyes were more open.

Inspired to bring this heightened awareness to your own strolls? See right for how to make walking a feast for the senses

STEP INTO THE SENSATIONS

- Beauty and harmony can be found outdoors, even when the weather and the surroundings are far from dreamy. Slowing down and focusing on what's around you can be effective ways of appreciating things that often pass unobserved.

- By asking yourself the question 'what is good about this moment?', you might find yourself noticing all manner of different things, from the overall mood of the landscape to subtle details. The longer you pause, the more you'll see.

- Walking has always been a gratifying (and free) way of thinking things out, so allow your mind to wander at will. But by shifting your attention back to the present – and the sights, sounds and smells that surround you – you'll often uncover rich rewards.

- Taking a stroll at an unusual time of day can be a brilliant way of experiencing a new side to a path you're familiar with. The light, the wildlife and the overall atmosphere can become markedly different.

- Learning the names and traits of the trees and birds you pass can be a hugely satisfying way of forging an even closer link with the outdoors. Walking without a mobile phone has obvious benefits, but on the flipside, there are apps that can help pick out birds by their calls and, if used sparingly, will help you to ID avian encounters.

- Concentrating your attention on watching a river flowing downstream, or the behaviour of birds or insects, can be an easy way of achieving a focused, meditative state of mind during a walk.

- Try to see each walk you take as a fresh adventure. What's the character of the wind today? And the sky? The clouds? How does the ground feel underfoot? What is there to spot that shows the passing of the seasons?

Words: **Ben Lerwill**

Do the shoes pinch?

Stepping into others' footwear offers an invaluable perspective, aiding empathy and understanding – but how often do you show yourself the same kindness?

Of all the emotional tools that aid connection with others, empathy is an interesting one, related to sympathy but different to kindness. Some are blessed with a capacity for it, even though many psychologists view it as a learned behaviour that can be cultivated throughout life. It can be defined as the ability to step into someone else's shoes – to see things from another's perspective, to slide, albeit temporarily, into a mould not made by you. Seeing the world from inside another shape helps to develop fellow feeling and lessens the divide between people. It could be viewed as a gift as it recognises standards are personal, and can't be met by all.

For some, however, empathy feels like a mandate – less of a gift and more an imperative. From the moment they're able, they cram their feet into other people's metaphorical footwear before they've tried on their own. In the rush to empathise with others, they forget to do the same for themselves. They've often no idea if their own shoes even fit, so quick are they to wear someone else's. Yet there can't be many people who haven't, on occasion, been their own harshest critic, picking apart each supposed fault and treating themselves in a way they'd never treat a friend. Self-focused kind understanding is hard. Yet maybe that tool for empathy – stepping into someone else's shoes – can be repurposed to aid inner resilience.

Trying on another's footwear means you first have to step out of your own. So how about, instead of hurriedly taking that option, you return – like a stranger – to yourself? Imagine if you could emerge from the shape you make, observe it kindly and climb back in with the warmth and understanding of a friend.

It's a radical idea – your comfort zone can often be to seek, and then criticise, every way in which you haven't matched up to your high ideals. If that's what you're used to, it might seem a challenge to become someone with whom you'd like to empathise. Yet this is what ought to be your mandate, for how can you discover that special sympathetic feeling for others, unless you've learned it for yourself?

Viewing the mould you make as if it belongs to a stranger might be the trick to unlocking a self-directed warmer heart. It could help you recognise that the ways you don't match up are only manifestations of past hurts or overblown expectations. Acknowledging that you're no more or less human than anyone else is essential for wellbeing. So, step out of your own shoes, then climb back into them as if they belonged to someone else. Show yourself, as you would with another, all the warmth and understanding in the world.

HOW TO STEP OUT OF – AND THEN BACK INTO – YOUR OWN SHOES

- Recall the last time you felt loving kindness towards another.
- Now imagine extending that emotion to yourself.
- Picture climbing out of your shoes, and looking back with the eyes of a friend.
- Now step back into your shape as if you were that friend.
- Give yourself a mental hug, knowing you merit as much warm understanding as anyone else.
- Make this a daily practice, and feel your self-empathy unfold.

Words: **Stephanie Lam**
Read more of Stephanie's thoughts on Instagram @Stephanie_Lam_1.